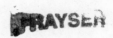

Prentice Hall ASE Test Preparation Series

Heating and Air Conditioning (A7)

James D. Halderman, Professor
Sinclair Community College
Dayton, Ohio
ASE Certified Master Automobile Technician
ASE Certified Advanced Level (L1)
ASE Certified Undercar Specialist
ASE Certified Master Engine Machinist

Chase D. Mitchell, Jr.
Utah Valley State College
Orem, Utah
ASE Certified Master Automobile Technician
ASE Certified Advanced Level (L1)

PEARSON
Prentice Hall

Upper Saddle River, New Jersey
Columbus, Ohio

Editor in Chief: Stephen Helba
Executive Editor: Ed Francis
Production Editor: Christine M. Buckendahl
Design Coordinator: Diane Ernsberger
Cover Designer: Jeff Vanik
Production Manager: Brian Fox
Marketing Manager: Mark Marsden

This book was printed and bound by Courier Kendallville. The cover was printed by Phoenix Color Corp.

Pearson Education Ltd.
Pearson Education Australia Pty. Limited
Pearson Education Singapore Pte. Ltd.
Pearson Education North Asia Ltd.
Pearson Education Canada, Ltd.
Pearson Educación de Mexico, S.A. de C.V.
Pearson Education—Japan
Pearson Education Malaysia Pte. Ltd.
Pearson Education, *Upper Saddle River, New Jersey*

10 9 8 7 6 5 4 3 2 1
ISBN: 0-13-019191-4

Table of Contents

Preface

This study guide was written to help service technicians and students of automotive technology prepare to take the National ASE Certification Tests. This study guide includes the following features:

- **Sample ASE-type test questions** organized and correlated to the ASE test task list

- **Answers with detailed explanations** of why the right answer is correct as well as why the wrong answers are not correct

- **Heavily-illustrated questions and explanations** which explain the questions and answers.

- **A CD ROM** that includes additional study questions with answers plus additional study material to help the reader gain the knowledge necessary to successfully pass the ASE Certification Test

- **A coupon for FREE access to a Web site** for additional test questions that are graded online as you complete each 10-question quiz

- **A comprehensive English and Spanish language glossary** that gives detailed definitions of all technical words and terms used in the ASE Certification Test

- **Two appendixes** that address ASE assumed knowledge of environmental/ hazardous material handling and safety issues.

- **An index** allowing key words or topics to be quickly located.

About the ASE Tests

What is ASE?

ASE is an abbreviation for the **National Institute for Automotive Service Excellence** (simply known as ASE), which was formed in 1972 to provide standardized testing of service technicians.

ASE is a nonprofit association, and its main goal is to improve the quality of vehicle service through testing and volunteer certification.

What areas of vehicle service are covered by the ASE tests?

Automobile test service areas include:

A1 Engine Repair
A2 Automatic Transmission/Transaxle
A3 Manual Drive Train and Axles
A4 Suspension and Steering
A5 Brakes
A6 Electrical/Electronic Systems
A7 Heating and Air Conditioning
A8 Engine Performance

If a technician takes and passes all eight of the automobile tests and has achieved two or more years of work experience, ASE will award the designation of **ASE Certified Master Automobile Technician.** Contact ASE for other certification areas.

How can I contact ASE?

ASE
101 Blue Seal Drive, SE
Suite 101
Leesburg, VA 20175

Toll free: 1-877-ASE-TECH (273-8324)
1-703-669-6600
Web site: www.asecert.org

When are the tests given and where?

The ASE tests are given at hundreds of test sites in early May and early November of each year. Deadline for registration is usually in late March for the May tests and in late September for the November tests. Consult the ASE registration booklet or Web site for details and locations of the test sites.

What do I have to do to register?

You can register for the ASE tests in three ways:

1. Mail in the registration form that is in the registration booklet.
2. Register online at www.asecert.org.
3. Telephone at (703) 669-6600

Call ASE toll-free at 1-877-273-8324 or visit the Web site for details about cost and dates.

How many years of work experience are needed?

ASE requires that you have two or more years of full-time, hands-on working experience either as an automobile, truck, truck equipment, or school bus technician, engine machinist, or in collision repair, refinishing, or damage analysis and estimating for certification, except as noted below. If you have *not* previously provided work experience information, you will receive a Work Experience Report Form with your admission ticket. You *must* complete and return this form to receive a certificate.

Substitutions for work experience. You may receive credit for up to one year of the two-year work experience requirement by substituting relevant formal training in one, or a combination, of the following:

High School Training: Three full years of training, either in automobile/truck/school bus repair or in collision repair, refinishing, or damage estimating, may be substituted for one year of work experience.

Post-High School Training: Two full years of post-high school training in a public or private trade school, technical institute, community or four-year college, or in an apprenticeship program may be counted as one year of work experience.

Short Courses: For shorter periods of post-high school training, you may substitute two months of training for one month of work experience.

You may receive full credit for the two-year work experience requirement with the following:

Completion of Apprenticeship: Satisfactory completion of either a three-or-four-year bona fide apprenticeship program.

Are there any hands-on activities on the ASE test?

No. All ASE tests are written using objective-type questions, meaning that you must select the correct answer from four possible alternatives.

Who writes the ASE questions?

All ASE test questions are written by a panel of industry experts, educators, and experienced ASE certified service technicians. Each question is reviewed by the committee and it is checked for the following:

- **Technically accurate.** All test questions use the correct terms and only test for vehicle manufacturer's recommended service procedures. Slang is not used nor are any aftermarket accessories included on the ASE test.

- **Manufacturer neutral.** All efforts are made to avoid using vehicle or procedures that are manufacturer specific such as to General Motors vehicles or to Toyotas. A service technician should feel comfortable about being able to answer the questions regardless of the type or brand of vehicle.

- **Logical answers.** All effort is made to be sure that all answers (not just the correct answers) are possible. While this may seem to make the test tricky, it is designed to test for real knowledge of the subject.

- **Random answer.** All efforts are made to be sure that the correct answers are not always the longest answer or that one letter, such as **c**, is not used more than any other letter.

What types of questions are asked on the ASE test?

All ASE test questions are objective. This means that there will not be questions where you will have to write an answer. Instead, all you have to do is select one of the four possible answers and place a mark in the correct place on the score sheet.

- **Multiple-choice questions**

  This type of question has one correct (or mostly correct) answer (called the key) and three incorrect answers (called distracters). A multiple-choice question example:

  What part of an automotive engine does not move?

  > a. Piston
  > b. Connecting rod
  > c. Block
  > d. Valve

The correct answer is **c** (block). This type of question asks for a specific answer. Answer **a** (piston), **b** (connecting rod), and **d** (valve) all move during normal engine operation. The best answer is **c** (block) because even though it may vibrate, it does not move as the other parts do.

- **Technician A and Technician B questions**

This type of question is generally considered to be the most difficult according to service technicians who take the ASE test. A situation or condition is usually stated and two technicians (A and B) say what they think could be the correct answer and you must decide which technician is correct.

 a. Technician A only
 b. Technician B only
 c. Both Technicians A and B
 d. Neither Technician A nor B

The best way to answer this type of question is to carefully read the question and consider Technician A and Technician B answers to be solutions to a true or false question. If Technician A is correct, mark on the test by Technician A the letter T for true. (Yes, you can write on the test.) If Technician B is also correct, write the letter T for true by Technician B. Then mark **c** on your test score sheet, for both technicians are correct.

Example:

Two technicians are discussing an engine that has lower than specified fuel pressure. Technician A says that the fuel pump could be the cause. Technician B says that the fuel pressure regulator could be the cause.

Which technician is correct?

 a. Technician A only
 b. Technician B only
 c. Both Technicians A and B
 d. Neither Technician A nor B

Analysis:

Is Technician A correct? The answer is yes because if the fuel pump was defective, the pump pressure could be lower than specified by the vehicle manufacturer. Is Technician B correct? The answer is yes because a stuck open or a regulator with a weak spring could be the cause of lower than specified fuel pressure. The correct answer is therefore **c** (Both Technicians A and B are correct).

- **Most-likely-type questions**

This type of question asks which of the four possible items listed is the most likely to cause the problem or symptom. This type of question is often considered to be difficult because recent experience may lead you to answer the question incorrectly because even though it is possible, it is not the "most likely."

Example:

Which of the items below is the most likely to cause blue exhaust at engine start?

a. Valve stem seals
b. Piston rings
c. Clogged PCV valve
d. A stuck oil pump regulator valve

Analysis:

The correct answer is **a** because valve stem seals are the most likely to cause this problem. Answer **b** is not correct because even though worn piston rings can cause the engine to burn oil and produce blue exhaust smoke, it is not the most likely cause of blue smoke at engine start. Answers **c** and **d** are not correct because even though these items could contribute to the engine burning oil and producing blue exhaust smoke, they are not the most likely.

- **Except-type questions**

ASE will sometimes use a question that includes answers that are all correct except one. You have to determine which of the four questions is not correct.

Example:

A radiator is being pressure tested using a hand-operated tester. This test will check for leaks in all except:

a. Radiator
b. Heater core
c. Water pump
d. Evaporator

Analysis:

The correct answer is **d** because the evaporator is not included in the cooling system and will not be pressurized during this test. Answers **a** (radiator), **b** (heater core), and **c** (water pump) are all being tested under pressure exerted on the cooling system by the pressure tester.

- **Least-likely-type questions**

  Another type of question asked on many ASE tests is a question that asks which of the following is least likely to be the cause of a problem or symptom. In other words, all of the answers are possible, but it is up to the reader to determine which answer is the least likely to be correct.

  Example:

  Which of the following is the least likely cause of low oil pressure?

  a. Clogged oil pump screen
  b. Worn main bearing
  c. Worn camshaft bearing
  d. Worn oil pump

  Analysis:

  The correct answer is **c** because even though worn camshaft bearings can cause low oil pressure, the other answers are more likely to be the cause.

Should I guess if I don't know the answer?

Yes. ASE tests simply record the correct answers, and by guessing, you will have at least a 25% (1 out of 4) chance. If you leave the answer blank, it will be scored as being incorrect. Instead of guessing entirely, try to eliminate as many of the answers as possible as not being very likely. If you can eliminate two out of the four, you have increased your chance of guessing to 50% (two out of four).

HINT: Never change an answer. Some research has shown that your first answer is most likely to be correct. It is human nature to read too much into the question rather than accept the question as it was written.

Is each test the same every time I take it?

No. ASE writes many questions for each area and selects from this "test bank" for each test session. You may see some of the same questions if you take the same test in the spring and then again in the fall, but you will also see many different questions.

Can I write or draw on the test form?

Yes. You may write or figure on the test, but do not write on the answer form or it can be misread during scanning and affect your score. You turn in your test and the answer form at the end of the session and the test is not reused.

Can I skip questions I don't know and come back to answer later?

Yes. You may skip a question if you wish, but be sure to mark the question and return to answer the question later. It is often recommended to answer the question or guess and go on with the test so that you do not run out of time to go back over the questions.

How much time do I have to take the tests?

All ASE test sessions are 4 hours and 15 minutes long. This is usually enough time for you to take up to four certification tests. ASE recommends that you do not attempt to take more than 225 questions or four tests at any one session. The ASE tests are spread over four days so it is possible to take all eight ASE test areas during a test period (spring or fall).

Will I have to know specifications and gauge readings?

Yes and no. You will be asked the correct range for a particular component or operation and you must know about what the specification should be. Otherwise, the questions will state that the value is less than or greater than the allowable specification. The question will deal with how the service technician should proceed or what action should be taken.

Can I take a break during the test?

Yes, you may use the restroom after receiving permission from the proctor of the test site.

Can I leave early if I have completed the test(s)?

Yes, you may leave quietly after you have completed the test(s). You must return the score sheet(s) and the test booklets as you leave.

How are the tests scored?

The ASE tests are machine scored and the results tabulated by American College Testing (ACT).

What percentage do I need to achieve to pass the ASE test?

While there is no exact number of questions that must be answered correctly in each area, an analysis of the test results indicate that the percentage needed to pass varies from 61% to 69%. Therefore, in order to pass the Heating and Air Conditioning (A7) ASE certification test, you will have to answer about 33 questions correct out of 50. In other words, you can miss about 17 questions and still pass.

What happens if I do not pass? Do I have to wait a year before trying again?

No. If you fail to achieve a passing score on any ASE test, you can take the test again at the next testing session (in May or November).

Do I have to pay another registration fee if I already paid it once?

Yes. The registration fee is due at every test session in May or November whether you select to take one or more ASE tests. Therefore, it is wise to take as many tests as you can at each test session.

How long do I have to wait to know the results?

You will receive written notice within two months after the test. Notification is sent out in July for the May test and in January for the November test sessions. You will be notified that you either "passed" a test(s) or that "more preparation is needed," meaning that you did not score high enough to pass the test and be rewarded with certification in the content area.

Will I receive notice of which questions I missed?

ASE sends out a summary of your test results, which shows how many questions you missed in each category, but not individual questions.

Will ASE send me the correct answers to the questions I missed so I will know how to answer them in the future?

No. ASE will not send you the answers to test questions.

Are the questions in this study guide actual ASE test questions?

No. The test questions on the actual ASE certification tests are copyrighted and cannot be used by others. The test questions in this study guide cover the same technical information and the question format is similar to the style used on the actual test.

Test Taking Tips

Start Now

Even if you have been working on vehicles for a long time, taking an ASE certification test can be difficult. The questions will not include how things work or other "textbook" knowledge. The questions are based on "real world" diagnosis and service. The tests may seem tricky to some because the "distracters" (the wrong answers) are designed to be similar to the correct answer.

If this is your first time taking the test or you are going to recertify, start now to prepare. Allocate time each day to study.

Practice Is Important

Many service technicians do not like taking tests. As a result, many technicians rush through the test to get the pain over with quickly. Also, many service technicians have lots of experiences on many different vehicles. This is what makes them good at what they do, but when an everyday problem is put into a question format (multiple choice), the answer may not be as clear as your experience has taught you.

Keys to Success

The key to successful test taking includes:

- Practice answering similar type questions.
- Carefully read each question two times to make sure you understand the question.
- Read each answer.
- Pick the best answer.
- Avoid reading too much into each question.
- Do not change an answer unless you are sure that the answer is definitely wrong.
- Look over the glossary of automotive terms for words that are not familiar to you.

The best preparation is practice, practice, and more practice. This is where using the ASE Test Prep practice tests can help.

Prepare Mentally

Practicing also helps relieve another potential problem many people have called "chronic test syndrome." This condition is basically an inability to concentrate or focus during a test. The slightest noise, fear of failure, and worries about other things all contribute. The best medicine is practice, practice, and more practice. With practice, test taking becomes almost second nature.

Prepare Physically

Be prepared physically. Get enough sleep and eat right.

One Month Before the Test

- Budget your time for studying. On average you will need 4 to 6 hours of study for each test that you are taking.
- Use the ASE Test Prep Online test preparation service three or more times a week for your practice.
- Study with a friend or a group if possible.

The Week Before the Test

- Studying should consist of about 2 hours of reviewing for each test being taken.
- Make sure you know how to get to the testing center. If possible drive to the test site and locate the room.
- Get plenty of rest.

The Day of the Test

- Study time is over.
- Keep your work schedule light or get the day off if possible.
- Eat a small light meal the evening of the test.
- Drink a large glass of water 1 to 2 hours before the test. (The brain and body work on electrical impulses, and water is used as a conductor.)
- Arrive at least 30 minutes early at the test center. Be ready to start on time.

What to Bring to the Test

- A photo ID.
- Your Entry Ticket that came with your ASE packet.
- Two sharpened #2 pencils.

During the Test

- BREATHE (oxygen is the most important nutrient for the brain.)
- Read every question TWICE.
- Read ALL the ANSWERS.
- If you have trouble with a question, leave it blank and continue. At the end of the test, go back and try any skipped questions. (Frequently, you will get a hint in another question that follows.)

Study Guide and ASE Test Correlation Chart

This ASE study guide is divided into the sub-content areas that correlate to the actual ASE certification test as follows:

Test Area Covered	Number of ASE Certification Test Questions	Number of Study Guide Questions
Heating and Air Conditioning (A7)	**50 total**	**110 total**
A. A/C System Diagnosis and Repair	12	34 (#1-#34*)
B. Refrigeration System Component Diagnosis and Repair	10	24 (#35-#58)
C. Heating and Engine Cooling Systems Diagnosis and Repair	5	20 (#59-#78)
D. Operating Systems and Related Controls Diagnosis and Repair	16	22 (#79-#100)
E. Refrigerant Recovery, Recycling and Handling	7	10 (#101-#110)

*The study guide questions are numbered consecutively to make it easier to locate the correct answers in the back of the book.

Heating and Air Conditioning (A7)

A. Air Conditioning System Diagnosis and Repair Questions

1. Both high-side pressures and low-side pressures are low with the engine running and the selector set to the air conditioning position. Technician A says that the system is undercharged. Technician B says the cooling fan could be inoperative. Which technician is correct?

    a. Technician A only
    b. Technician B only
    c. Both Technicians A and B
    d. Neither Technician A nor B

2. Technician A says that an expansion valve can be tested using a CO_2 fire extinguisher to check if the cold will cause the valve to close. Technician B says that the operation of the orifice tube can be tested using a CO_2 fire extinguisher to cool the orifice tube and watching for a drop in low-side pressure. Which technician is correct?

    a. Technician A only
    b. Technician B only
    c. Both Technicians A and B
    d. Neither Technician A nor B

3. A lack of cooling is being diagnosed. A technician discovers that the high-pressure line is hot to the touch on both sides of the orifice tube. Technician A says that is normal operation for an orifice tube system. Technician B says that the orifice tube may be clogged. Which technician is correct?

    a. Technician A only
    b. Technician B only
    c. Both Technicians A and B
    d. Neither Technician A nor B

4. Frost is observed on the line between the condenser and the receiver/drier. Technician A says that this is normal if the air conditioning were being operated on a hot and humid day. Technician B says that a restriction in the line or at the outlet of the condenser could be the cause. Which technician is correct?

    a. Technician A only
    b. Technician B only
    c. Both Technicians A and B
    d. Neither Technician A nor B

5. The discharge air temperature is warm and the pressure gauges shown represent which *most likely* cause?

   a. Low on refrigerant
   b. Lack of airflow through the condenser
   c. Defective compressor
   d. Icing of the evaporator

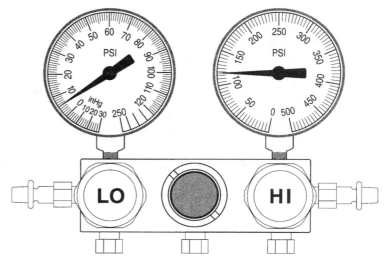

6. The airflow from the vents slows down after the vehicle has been driven for a while and the pressure gauges shown represent which *most likely* cause?

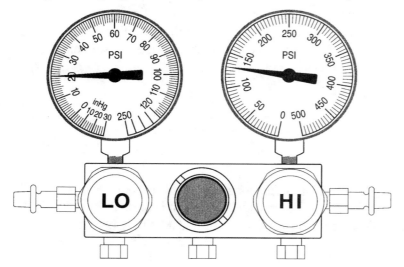

   a. Low on refrigerant
   b. Lack of airflow through the condenser
   c. Defective compressor
   d. Icing of the evaporator

7. The discharge air temperature is warm and the pressure gauges shown represent which *most likely* cause?

   a. Overcharged with refrigerant
   b. Restricted liquid line or low on refrigerant
   c. Lack of airflow through the condenser
   d. Defective compressor

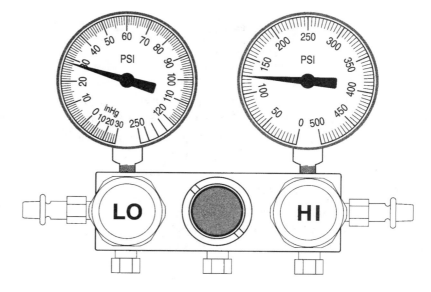

8. The discharge air temperature is cool and the pressure gauges shown represent which *most likely* cause?

    a. Low on refrigerant
    b. Clogged condensate drain
    c. Excess refrigerant in the system
    d. Lack of airflow through the condenser

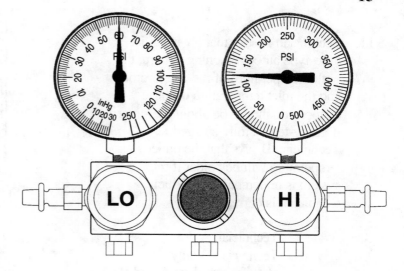

9. The discharge air temperature is warm or slightly cool. The pressure gauges shown represent which *most likely* cause?

    a. Low on refrigerant
    b. Defective compressor
    c. Excess refrigerant in the system
    d. Lack of airflow through the condenser

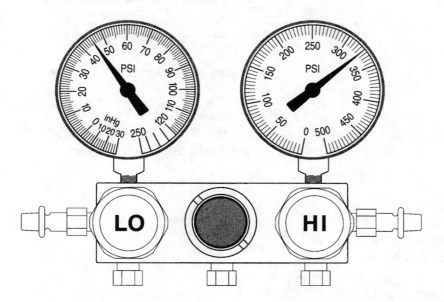

10. The owner of a vehicle equipped with an orifice tube-type air conditioning system complains that the inside of the vehicle does not cool properly. The air conditioning compressor clutch constantly cycles on and off whenever the air conditioning is on. Technician A says that the system is likely discharged. Technician B says that the most likely cause is an electrical short in the wiring to the air conditioning compressor clutch. Which technician is correct?

    a. Technician A only
    b. Technician B only
    c. Both Technicians A and B
    d. Neither Technician A nor B

11. Technician A says that on an orifice tube-type air conditioning system, the outlet temperature of the evaporator and the inlet temperature of the evaporator should be about the same if the system is fully charged. Technician B says that the outlet temperature will be colder if the system is undercharged. Which technician is correct?

    a. Technician A only
    b. Technician B only
    c. Both Technicians A and B
    d. Neither Technician A nor B

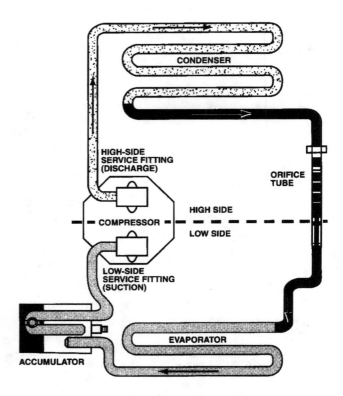

ORIFICE-TUBE SYSTEM

12. A customer states that the vehicle does not cool as well as it should. Technician A says that the system could be low on charge. Technician B says that if the electric radiator cooling fan is not functioning, this can cause a lack of cooling inside the vehicle. Which technician is correct?

    a. Technician A only
    b. Technician B only
    c. Both Technicians A and B
    d. Neither Technician A nor B

13. An automotive air conditioning system is being tested for a lack-of-cooling complaint. Both high and low pressures are higher than normal. Technician A says that the system is low on charge. Technician B says that the system is overcharged. Which technician is correct?

    a. Technician A only
    b. Technician B only
    c. Both Technicians A and B
    d. Neither Technician A nor B

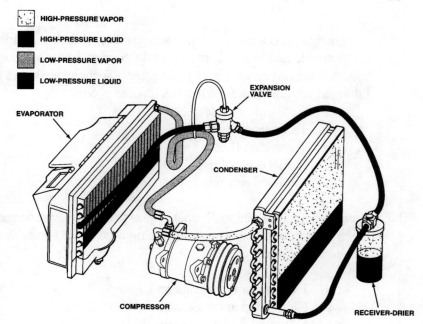

HIGH-PRESSURE VAPOR
HIGH-PRESSURE LIQUID
LOW-PRESSURE VAPOR
LOW-PRESSURE LIQUID

EVAPORATOR
EXPANSION VALVE
CONDENSER
COMPRESSOR
RECEIVER-DRIER

14. Technician A says that the low-side pressure of the air conditioning system is best checked for leaks with the engine off. Technician B says that the low side of the system is best checked for leaks when the engine is on and the system is operating. Which technician is correct?

    a. Technician A only
    b. Technician B only
    c. Both Technicians A and B
    d. Neither Technician A nor B

15. The high-side pressure is higher than normal. Technician A says that the compressor may be defective. Technician B says that the condenser may be clogged with leaves or other debris blocking the airflow. Which technician is correct?

    a. Technician A only
    b. Technician B only
    c. Both Technicians A and B
    d. Neither Technician A nor B

16. A customer complained of a clear liquid leaking from underneath the vehicle on the passenger side after driving for a short time with the air conditioning on. The problem only occurs when the air conditioner is operating. Technician A says that the evaporator may be leaking. Technician B says that this may be normal condensed water formed on the cold evaporator coil. Which technician is correct?

    a. Technician A only
    b. Technician B only
    c. Both Technicians A and B
    d. Neither Technician A nor B

17. Both the low and the high pressure are within normal ranges, yet the inside of the vehicle is not cooling. Technician A says that a partially clogged orifice tube could be the cause. Technician B says that too much refrigerant oil in the system could be the cause. Which technician is correct?

    a. Technician A only
    b. Technician B only
    c. Both Technicians A and B
    d. Neither Technician A nor B

18. A technician is observing the pressure gauges when the engine is turned off and notices that the high-side and low-side pressures do not equalize quickly as they should. Technician A says that the orifice tube may be clogged. Technician B says that the desiccant may be saturated with moisture. Which technician is correct?

    a. Technician A only
    b. Technician B only
    c. Both Technicians A and B
    d. Neither Technician A nor B

19. A customer states that the carpet on the floor on the passenger side is wet and noticed this when the air conditioning was first being used in the spring during damp weather. Which is the *most likely* cause?

    a. Evaporator refrigerant leak
    b. Clogged evaporator case drain
    c. Saturated desiccant in the drier
    d. Clogged screen in the accumulator

20. What two items *must* be installed or replaced when retrofitting a CFC-12 system to an HFC-134a system?

    a. Fittings and a label
    b. Compressor and O-rings
    c. Label and the condenser
    d. Fittings and the drier

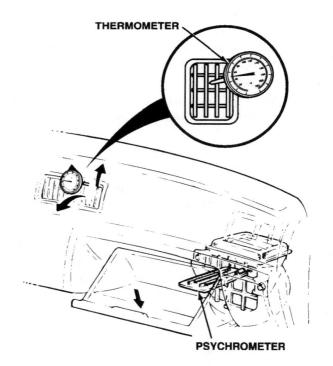

21. A thermometer inserted into the A/C vents reads 44°F in the right and center vents, but 52°F in the left (driver) side vent. What is the *most likely* cause?

    a. Too much oil charge in the system
    b. A partially restricted orifice tube
    c. A misadjusted blend door
    d. A disconnected vent tube

22. Two technicians are discussing if a 1993 vehicle is equipped with a R-12 or a R-134a system. Technician A says that this information should be on an underhood label. Technician B says that the size and shape of the fittings can be used to help determine what refrigerant is in the system. Which technician is correct?

    a. Technician A only
    b. Technician B only
    c. Both Technicians A and B
    d. Neither Technician A nor B

23. An air conditioning performance test is being performed. All of the following should be done *except*

    a. Turn blower to high speed
    b. Open the doors
    c. Set the controls for maximum cooling
    d. Place a thermometer in the recirculation door vent

24. Two technicians are discussing refrigerant oil. Technician A says that PAG oil comes in more than one viscosity and that using the wrong thickness of oil could cause damage to the compressor. Technician B says that refrigerant oil must be kept in a sealed container. Which technician is correct?

    a. Technician A only
    b. Technician B only
    c. Both Technicians A and B
    d. Neither Technician A nor B

25. A vehicle is being checked for a lack of cooling concern about two months after another shop had replaced the compressor. Technician A says that debris from the old compressor could have clogged the orifice tube. Technician B says that the system could be low on charge due to a leak in the system. Which technician is correct?

    a. Technician A only
    b. Technician B only
    c. Both Technicians A and B
    d. Neither Technician A nor B

26. The air flows from the heater (floor) and defroster (windshield) ducts all of the time regardless of the position of the heater/air-conditioning mode control. Which is the *most likely* cause?

    a. A disconnected vacuum hose from the intake manifold
    b. A defective heater/air-conditioning mode control unit
    c. Air-conditioning system is discharged
    d. A stuck blend door

27. Two technicians are discussing leak testing of an air-conditioning system. Technician A says that the blower motor resistor pack can be removed to test the evaporator for possible leaks using a leak detector. Technician B says to check the evaporator for leaks at the condensate drain. Which technician is correct?

    a. Technician A only
    b. Technician B only
    c. Both Technicians A and B
    d. Neither Technician A nor B

28. An engine runs OK until the air conditioning is engaged. Then it idles roughly and occasionally stalls. What is the *most likely* cause?

    a. A shorted ECT sensor
    b. A stuck idle air control (IAC)
    c. A clogged orifice tube
    d. The air-conditioning system is overcharged

29. The air-conditioning system seems to be functioning correctly, but it does not cool as fast or as cold as a similar model. Which is the *least likely* cause?

    a. Debris clogged condenser
    b. Low on refrigerant charge
    c. Partially clogged orifice tube
    d. Partially clogged condensate drain

30. A lack of cooling is being diagnosed. On an 80°F (27°C) day, both low and high pressure gauges read 87 psi (600 kPa). Technician A says that a clogged orifice tube is the *most likely* cause. Technician B says that the system is low on refrigerant charge. Which technician is correct?

    a. Technician A only
    b. Technician B only
    c. Both Technicians A and B
    d. Neither Technician A nor B

31. A lack of cooling is being diagnosed after the system was retrofitted to R-134a. The high side pressure is higher than normal and the compressor feels cool when touched. What is the *most likely* cause?

    a. A lack of oil in the system
    b. Undercharged with refrigerant
    c. Overcharged with refrigerant
    d. Clogged or restricted condenser

32. The discharge line from the compressor is hot to the touch. Technician A says that the system is low on refrigerant. Technician B says that the compressor is worn and is not compressing the refrigerant enough for proper operation of the air-conditioning system. Which technician is correct?

    a. Technician A only
    b. Technician B only
    c. Both Technicians A and B
    d. Neither Technician A nor B

33. An R-12 system equipped with a sight glass is being diagnosed. Bubbles (foam) are observed all of the time the system is working with the doors open and the blower fan speed set to high. Which is the *most likely* cause?

    a. The system is empty of refrigerant – just air is in the system
    b. The system is low on refrigerant
    c. The system is overcharged with refrigerant
    d. There is water in the system

34. A strong pungent odor comes out of the air-conditioning vents. Technician A says that mouthwash should be poured into the air inlet near the windshield to stop the odor. Technician B says that fungicide should be sprayed onto the evaporator to stop the odor. Which technician is correct?

    a. Technician A only
    b. Technician B only
    c. Both Technicians A and B
    d. Neither Technician A nor B

Heating and Air Conditioning (A7)

B. Refrigeration System Component Diagnosis and Repair Questions

35. Technician A says that all HFC-134a systems use the same refrigerant oil. Technician B says that refrigerant oil, regardless of type, must be kept in a sealed container to keep it from absorbing moisture from the air. Which technician is correct?

    a. Technician A only
    b. Technician B only
    c. Both Technicians A and B
    d. Neither Technician A nor B

36. A front-wheel drive vehicle has a broken condenser line. What other vehicle component may also be defective that could have caused the condenser line to break?

    a. A shock absorber
    b. An engine mount
    c. A cooling fan
    d. An air-conditioning compressor drive belt

37. Two technicians are discussing the replacement of an air-conditioning compressor clutch. Technician A says that the air gap should be adjusted. Technician B says the front compressor seal should also be replaced whenever replacing the clutch assembly. Which technician is correct?

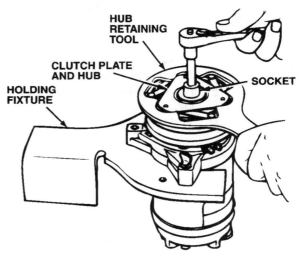

    a. Technician A only
    b. Technician B only
    c. Both Technicians A and B
    d. Neither Technician A nor B

38. Technician A says that the air-conditioning compressor should operate when the controls are set to the heat position. Technician B says the air-conditioning compressor should operate when the controls are set to the defrost position. Which technician is correct?

    a. Technician A only
    b. Technician B only
    c. Both Technicians A and B
    d. Neither Technician A nor B

39. The air-conditioning compressor clutch does not engage when the air-conditioning mode is selected and the engine is running. Technician A says that the system may be low on refrigerant charge. Technician B says the low-pressure switch may be electrically open. Which technician is correct?

    a. Technician A only
    b. Technician B only
    c. Both Technicians A and B
    d. Neither Technician A nor B

40. An air-conditioning compressor is noisy whenever the clutch is engaged. Technician A says that the drive belt may be defective. Technician B says the compressor may be defective. Which technician is correct?

    a. Technician A only
    b. Technician B only
    c. Both Technicians A and B
    d. Neither Technician A nor B

41. An oily area is discovered around the front clutch assembly of the air-conditioning compressor. Technician A says that the clutch is defective. Technician B says that the compressor seal could be leaking. Which technician is correct?

    a. Technician A only
    b. Technician B only
    c. Both Technicians A and B
    d. Neither Technician A nor B

42. Technician A says that some refrigerant oil should be added to a replacement condenser to make sure that the system has the correct amount of oil. Technician B says that a specified viscosity of oil must be used to ensure proper lubrication of the compressor. Which technician is correct?

    a. Technician A only
    b. Technician B only
    c. Both Technicians A and B
    d. Neither Technician A nor B

43. A condenser is being flushed. Technician A says that the old refrigerant oil can be mixed with and disposed of with used engine oil. Technician B says that mineral oil refrigerant should be added to the new condenser in a R-134a system. Which technician is correct?

    a. Technician A only
    b. Technician B only
    c. Both Technicians A and B
    d. Neither Technician A nor B

44. Technician A says that if an evaporator has been replaced, 2 or 3 ounces of refrigerant oil should be added to the system. Technician B says that the old evaporator should be drained and the oil measured to determine how much oil to add when installing the replacement evaporator. Which technician is correct?

   a. Technician A only
   b. Technician B only
   c. Both Technicians A and B
   d. Neither Technician A nor B

45. Two technicians are discussing orifice tubes. Technician A says the inlet screen should be installed facing the evaporator inlet. Technician B says the inlet screen should be installed facing toward the condenser section of the system. Which technician is correct?

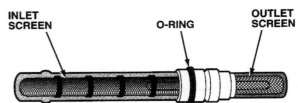

   a. Technician A only
   b. Technician B only
   c. Both Technicians A and B
   d. Neither Technician A nor B

46. A noisy compressor is being discussed. Technician A says that the air-conditioning system could be low on lubricating oil. Technician B says that the system could be overcharged. Which technician is correct?

   a. Technician A only
   b. Technician B only
   c. Both Technicians A and B
   d. Neither Technician A nor B

47. Both pressure gauge needles are oscillating rapidly. Which component is the *most likely* cause?

   a. The compressor (reed valves)
   b. The orifice tube (clogged)
   c. The expansion valve (stuck closed)
   d. The drier (desiccant bag is saturated with moisture)

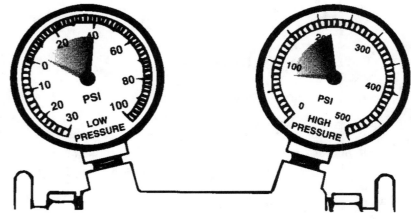

48. What is being measured?

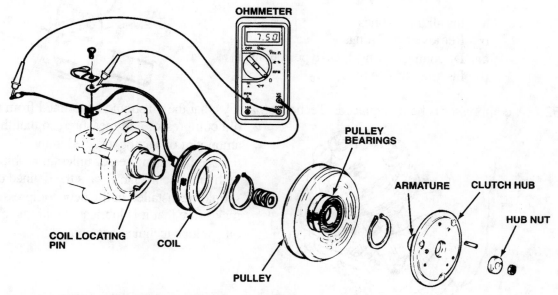

a. Available voltage at the compressor clutch
b. Voltage drop of the compressor clutch circuit
c. Capacitance of the radio suppressor
d. Resistance of the compressor clutch coil

49. What is this technician doing?

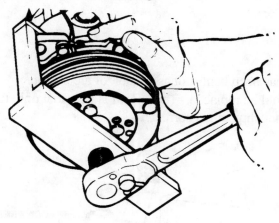

a. Installing the compressor drive pulley
b. Removing the compressor clutch assembly
c. Aligning the compressor drive pulley with the engine pulley
d. Separating the two halves of the compressor drive pulley

50. This special tool is being used to remove or install what air-conditioning component?

a. Low-pressure cut-off switch
b. High-pressure cut-off switch
c. Liquid line O-ring seal
d. Orifice tube

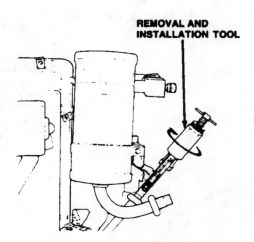

51. This special tool is used to perform what function?

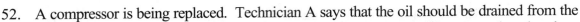

    a. Install the O-rings
    b. Remove the O-rings
    c. Disconnect spring-lock-type couplings
    d. Insert an orifice tube

52. A compressor is being replaced. Technician A says that the oil should be drained from the old compressor and measured so that the same amount of oil can be installed in the replacement compressor unless it is shipped with oil. Technician B says the drained oil should be installed in the new compressor to make sure that it is lubricated with the correct oil. Which technician is correct?

    a. Technician A only
    b. Technician B only
    c. Both Technicians A and B
    d. Neither Technician A nor B

53. The capillary tube on the expansion valve has been bent shut as a result of a collision. Technician A says the expansion valve should be replaced. Technician B says that only the capillary tube needs to be replaced. Which technician is correct?

    a. Technician A only
    b. Technician B only
    c. Both Technicians A and B
    d. Neither Technician A nor B

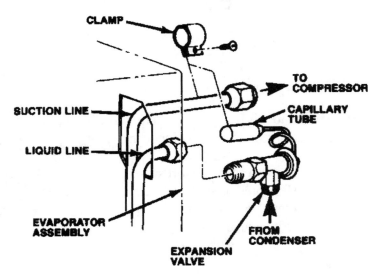

54. An automotive air-conditioning system has been disconnected for several months and is now being returned to service. Technician A says that the receiver drier or accumulator should be replaced. Technician B says the system should be flushed and fresh refrigerant oil should be installed before evacuating and recharging the system. Which technician is correct?

    a. Technician A only
    b. Technician B only
    c. Both Technicians A and B
    d. Neither Technician A nor B

55. A leaking evaporator is being replaced. Technician A says that 2 ounces or 3 ounces of refrigerant oil should be added to the new evaporator to allow for the amount that is trapped in the old evaporator. Technician B says that the condensate drain hole should be checked to see that it is open before completing the repair. Which technician is correct?

    a. Technician A only
    b. Technician B only
    c. Both Technicians A and B
    d. Neither Technician A nor B

56. A compressor clutch does not engage even when a jumper wire is connected directly to the compressor connection. An ohmmeter check of the compressor clutch coil results in a reading of 14.7 kΩ. Technician A says the compressor clutch coil is OK and that the compressor itself is defective. Technician B says the compressor clutch coil is defective. Which technician is correct?

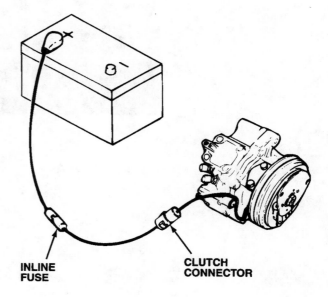

INLINE FUSE   CLUTCH CONNECTOR

    a. Technician A only
    b. Technician B only
    c. Both Technicians A and B
    d. Neither Technician A nor B

57. A replacement compressor clutch is being installed. All of the following should be checked *except:*

    a. Air gap
    b. Front seal leakage
    c. Drive belt
    d. Amount of refrigerant oil in the compressor

58. A clogged orifice tube is being replaced. Technician A says that the specified orifice tube should be used as a replacement because the orifice size can vary among the manufacturers. Technician B says that orifice tubes are sized by the outside diameter and that any orifice tube that fits will work OK. Which technician is correct?

    a. Technician A only
    b. Technician B only
    c. Both Technicians A and B
    d. Neither Technician A nor B

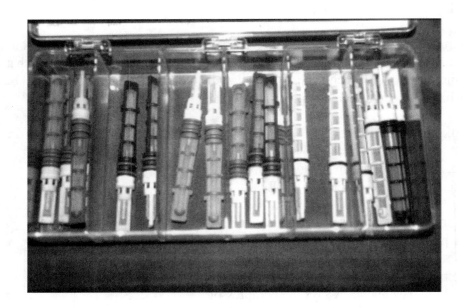

Heating and Air Conditioning (A7)

C. Heating and Engine Cooling Systems Diagnosis and Repair Questions

59. After the water pump was replaced and the cooling system refilled with coolant, the heater stopped providing hot air. Which is the *most likely* cause?

    a. The wrong concentration of antifreeze was installed
    b. An air pocket is trapped in the heater core
    c. A defective heater control valve
    d. A slipping water pump drive belt

60. A customer complained that the heat from the heater would come and go and vary with engine speed. What is the *most likely* cause?

    a. A defective thermostat
    b. A low coolant level
    c. A defective water (coolant) pump
    d. Incorrect antifreeze and water ratio

61. A service technician is replacing a water (coolant) pump. Technician A says that used coolant should be kept for recycling. Technician B says that the used coolant should be reused to refill the cooling system after the repair is completed. Which technician is correct?

    a. Technician A only
    b. Technician B only
    c. Both Technicians A and B
    d. Neither Technician A nor B

62. A customer complained of lack of heat from the heater. A check of the cooling system shows that the upper radiator hose is not getting hot. Technician A says that the thermostat may be defective (stuck open). Technician B says that the cause could be a defective (always engaged) thermostat cooling fan. Which technician is correct?

    a. Technician A only
    b. Technician B only
    c. Both Technicians A and B
    d. Neither Technician A nor B

63. A lack of heat from the heater is being diagnosed. Which is the *most likely* cause?

    a. A partially clogged radiator
    b. Hoses reversed on the heater core
    c. A partially clogged heater core
    d. A defective water pump

64. The temperature gauge approaches the red part of the temperature gauge (260°F or 127°C) if driven at slow speeds but does not overheat if driven at highway speeds. What is the *most likely* cause?

    a. Low coolant level
    b. Incorrect antifreeze/water mixture
    c. Defective water (coolant) pump
    d. Inoperative cooling fan

65. The coolant in a radiator froze when the temperature dropped to -20°F (-29°C). Technician A says that the 100% pure antifreeze in the cooling system could be the cause. Technician B says that too much water in the antifreeze could be the cause. Which technician is correct?

    a. Technician A only
    b. Technician B only
    c. Both Technicians A and B
    d. Neither Technician A nor B

66. The procedure that should be used when refilling an empty cooling system includes the following: _____.

    a. Determine capacity, then fill the cooling system halfway with antifreeze and the rest of the way with water.
    b. Fill completely with antifreeze, but mix a 50/50 solution for the overflow bottle.
    c. Fill the block and one-half of the radiator with 100% pure antifreeze and fill the rest of the radiator with water.
    d. Fill the radiator with antifreeze, start the engine, drain the radiator, and refill with 50/50 mixture of antifreeze and water.

67. An engine coolant temperature is measured to be 210°F (100°C) even though the thermostat specification states that a 195° unit is installed in the vehicle. Technician A says the thermostat is defective. Technician B says that the radiator is clogged causing the temperature to be higher than normal. Which technician is correct?

    a. Technician A only
    b. Technician B only
    c. Both Technicians A and B
    d. Neither Technician A nor B

68. Technician A says that the radiator should always be inspected for leaks and proper flow before installing a rebuilt engine. Technician B says that overheating during slow city driving can be due to a defective electric cooling fan. Which technician is correct?

    a. Technician A only
    b. Technician B only
    c. Both Technicians A and B
    d. Neither Technician A nor B

69. The "hot" light on the dash is being discussed by two technicians. Technician A says that the light comes on if the cooling system temperature is too high for safe operation of the engine. Technician B says that the light comes on whenever there is a decrease (drop) in cooling system pressure. Which technician is correct?

    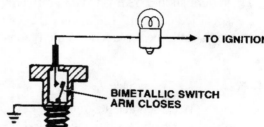

    a. Technician A only
    b. Technician B only
    c. Both Technicians A and B
    d. Neither Technician A nor B

70. A customer complains that the heater works sometimes, but sometimes only cold air comes out while driving. Technician A says that the water pump is defective. Technician B says that the cooling system could be low on coolant. Which technician is correct?

    a. Technician A only
    b. Technician B only
    c. Both Technicians A and B
    d. Neither Technician A nor B

71. Normal operating temperature is reached when _____.

    a. The radiator cap releases coolant into the overflow
    b. The upper radiator hose is hot and pressurized
    c. The electric cooling fan has cycled at least once (if the vehicle is so equipped)
    d. Either b or c occur

72. A cooling system is being refilled following a repair. Technician A says to use conventional green antifreeze (ethylene glycol-based with silicate and phosphate additives) regardless of the type of coolant originally in the system. Technician B says to refill the system with the coolant specified for use by the vehicle manufacturer. Which technician is correct?

    a. Technician A only
    b. Technician B only
    c. Both Technicians A and B
    d. Neither Technician A nor B

73. The windshield will not defog even though the defroster and/or the air-conditioning system seems to be functioning correctly. What is the *most likely* cause?

    a. A leaking heater core
    b. A leaking evaporator
    c. A stuck blend door
    d. Low on refrigerant charge

74. This radiator cap was discovered during routine service. Technician A says that the cooling system should be flushed and refilled with the specified coolant. Technician B says that the cap should be replaced. Which technician is correct?

    a. Technician A only
    b. Technician B only
    c. Both Technicians A and B
    d. Neither Technician A nor B

75. The upper radiator hose collapses when the engine is turned off. Which is the *most likely* cause?

    a. A defective radiator cap
    b. A defective upper radiator hose
    c. A clogged radiator
    d. A low coolant level

76. A thermostatic clutch is leaking fluid. Technician A says that the unit should be replaced. Technician B says that it can cause the engine to overheat. Which technician is correct?

    a. Technician A only
    b. Technician B only
    c. Both Technicians A and B
    d. Neither Technician A nor B

77. The water pump shown was removed from an engine that was running too hot. Technician A says that the cooling system should be flushed before being refilled with coolant. Technician B says that the specified coolant should be used to help avoid failure of the replacement pump. Which technician is correct?

    a. Technician A only
    b. Technician B only
    c. Both Technicians A and B
    d. Neither Technician A nor B

78. A pressure gauge is installed on the radiator filler neck and the system pressurized to 15 psi. After a few minutes, the pressure was down to 5 psi according to the gauge on the tester. What is the *least likely* cause?

    a. A leaking water pump
    b. A leaking evaporator
    c. A leaking radiator hose
    d. A leaking heater core

Heating and Air Conditioning (A7)

D. Operating System and Related Controls Diagnosis and Repair Questions

79. Technician A says that the air conditioning compressor clutch may not engage if the steering wheel is being turned sharply and the vehicle is equipped with power steering. Technician B says that the air conditioning compressor clutch may not engage if the refrigerant system is low on charge. Which technician is correct?

   a. Technician A only
   b. Technician B only
   c. Both Technicians A and B
   d. Neither Technician A nor B

80. The air from the blower motor goes mostly to the defrost ducts regardless of the position of the controls. Technician A says that the recirculation door may be stuck. Technician B says that the vacuum source for the mode doors may be leaking. Which technician is correct?

   a. Technician A only
   b. Technician B only
   c. Both Technicians A and B
   d. Neither Technician A nor B

81. A "pop" is heard from the radio speakers occasionally when the defroster or air conditioning is selected. Technician A says that the compressor clutch clamping diode may be blown. Technician B says that the air conditioning compressor clutch may have a poor electrical ground connection. Which technician is correct?

   a. Technician A only
   b. Technician B only
   c. Both Technicians A and B
   d. Neither Technician A nor B

82. A reduced amount of airflow from the air conditioning vents is being discussed. Technician A says that the evaporator could be clogged as a result of a small refrigerant leak causing oil to trap and hold dirt. Technician B says that the blower motor ground connection could have excessive voltage drop. Which technician is correct?

   a. Technician A only
   b. Technician B only
   c. Both Technicians A and B
   d. Neither Technician A nor B

83. Technician A says that an electrical open in the low-pressure switch can prevent the compressor from working. Technician B says that the compressor may not operate at low outside temperatures depending on the pressure sensed by the low-pressure switch. Which technician is correct?

    a. Technician A only
    b. Technician B only
    c. Both Technicians A and B
    d. Neither Technician A nor B

84. Technician A says that the voltage to the air conditioning compressor may be turned off on some vehicles when accelerating rapidly. Technician B says that a fault in the power steering pressure switch could prevent the air conditioning compressor from operating. Which technician is correct?

    a. Technician A only
    b. Technician B only
    c. Both Technicians A and B
    d. Neither Technician A nor B

85. An automatic air conditioning system is being diagnosed for cooler than the set temperature. Technician A says that a blocked inside air temperature sensor could be the cause. Technician B says that a blocked sun load sensor could be the cause. Which technician is correct?

    a. Technician A only
    b. Technician B only
    c. Both Technicians A and B
    d. Neither Technician A nor B

86. What is the meter measuring?

    a. Resistance of the ECT sensor
    b. Voltage signal of the ECT sensor
    c. Voltage output from the PCM
    d. Resistance of the electrical connector

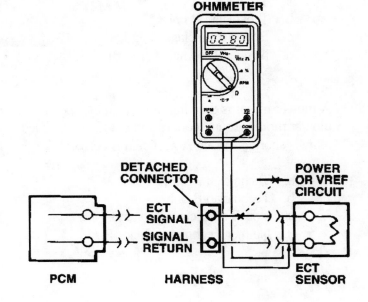

87. An HVAC relay is being checked using a DMM set to read ohms. Technician A says the relay being tested is OK. Technician B says the relay being tested is defective (open). Which technician is correct?

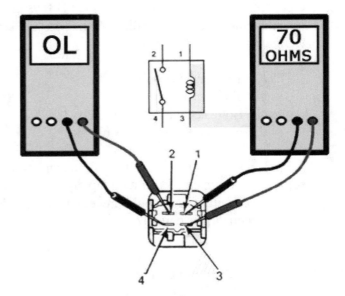

    a. Technician A only
    b. Technician B only
    c. Both Technicians A and B
    d. Neither Technician A nor B

88. A blower motor stopped working on all speeds. A technician tested the motor touching a jumper wire from the battery positive (+) terminal to the motor power terminal and the motor did run. Technician A says that the motor should be checked using a fused jumper lead to test for excessive current draw. Technician B says that the resistor pack and/or relay are likely to be defective. Which technician is correct?

    a. Technician A only
    b. Technician B only
    c. Both Technicians A and B
    d. Neither Technician A nor B

89. A blower motor is drawing more than the specified current. Technician A says that the blower motor ground connection could be corroded. Technician B says that the blower relay is shorted. Which technician is correct?

    a. Technician A only
    b. Technician B only
    c. Both Technicians A and B
    d. Neither Technician A nor B

90. The A/C compressor clutch does not engage. Technician A says that an open high pressure cutout switch could be the problem. Technician B says a blown compressor clutch diode could be the cause. Which technician is correct?

    a. Technician A only
    b. Technician B only
    c. Both Technicians A and B
    d. Neither Technician A nor B

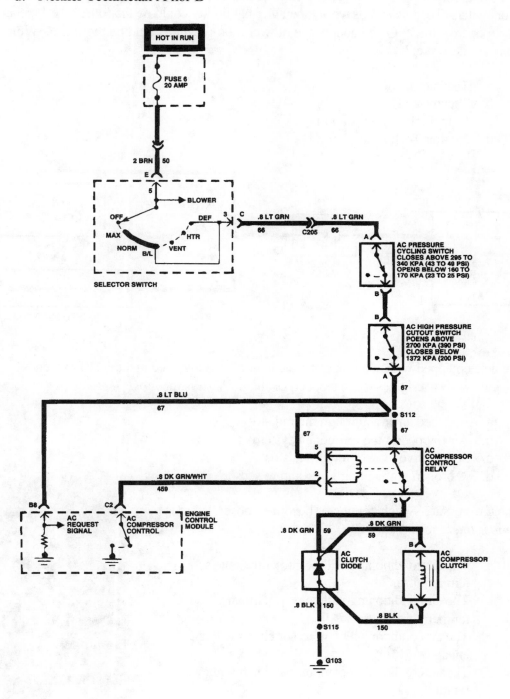

91. A blower is running slowly on all speeds. What is the *most likely* cause?

    a. A blown resistor
    b. Worn/dry bearings in the motor
    c. A bad fan switch
    d. Open ignition switch

92. The blower motor operates at low speed regardless of the position selected on the blower motor switch. Technician A says an open thermal limiter could be the cause. Technician B says an open at the "LO" contact of the blower motor switch could be the cause. Which technician is correct?

    a. Technician A only
    b. Technician B only
    c. Both Technicians A and B
    d. Neither Technician A nor B

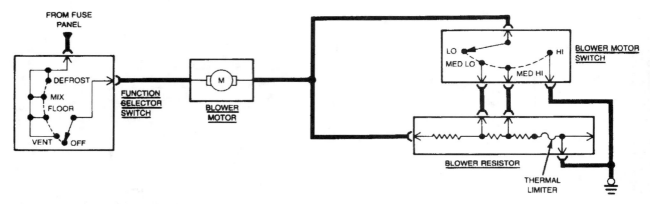

93. A vehicle equipped with automatic climate control was involved in a minor front-end collision. Afterward the system stopped cooling. What is the *most likely* cause?

    a. Reduced airflow through the radiator
    b. Air trapped in the refrigerant system
    c. A defective blower motor resistor
    d. A broken ambient air temperature sensor

94. The high-pressure switch connector becomes loose. What is the *most likely* result?

    a. The air conditioning will be cooler than the set temperature
    b. The air conditioning will be warmer than the set temperature
    c. The air conditioning compressor clutch will not engage
    d. The air conditioning compressor clutch will cycle rapidly

95. Two technicians are discussing the schematic shown. Technician A says that all three switches must be closed before the air-conditioning compressor clutch will engage. Technician B says that the low-pressure switch is closed when the system pressure is very low (almost zero psi). Which technician is correct?

   a. Technician A only
   b. Technician B only
   c. Both Technicians A and B
   d. Neither Technician A nor B

CYCLING-CLUTCH SWITCH

AC COMPRESSOR

12V

AC AND HEATER SWITCH

LOW-PRESSURE SWITCH

96. What service check is being performed?

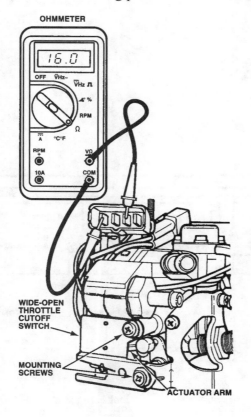

OHMMETER

16.0

OFF V̄Hz~ V̄Hz ⊓

⚡ %
RPM
Ω
A   °C°F
RPM   VΩ
10A   COM

WIDE-OPEN THROTTLE CUTOFF SWITCH

MOUNTING SCREWS

ACTUATOR ARM

   a. Checking the voltage of the throttle switch
   b. Checking the continuity of the wide-open-throttle switch
   c. Measuring the current flow through the throttle cutoff switch
   d. Measuring the resistance of the compressor clutch coil

97. The defroster does not work. Technician A says that the HVAC control head unit could be the cause. Technician B says that a fault in the defroster solenoid could be the cause. Which technician is correct?

    a. Technician A only
    b. Technician B only
    c. Both Technicians A and B
    d. Neither Technician A nor B

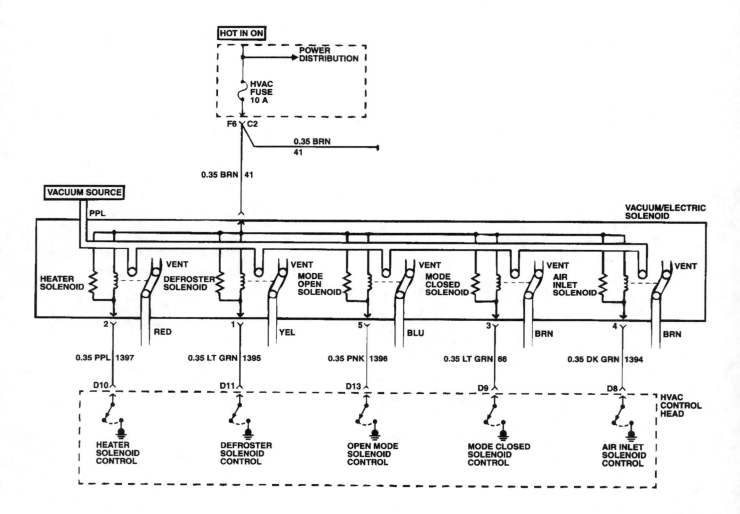

98. Where is the airflow being directed in the figure shown?

    a. Vent position
    b. Recirculation, dash vents
    c. Upper vent, air-conditioning vents
    d. Heat/defrost position, lower vents

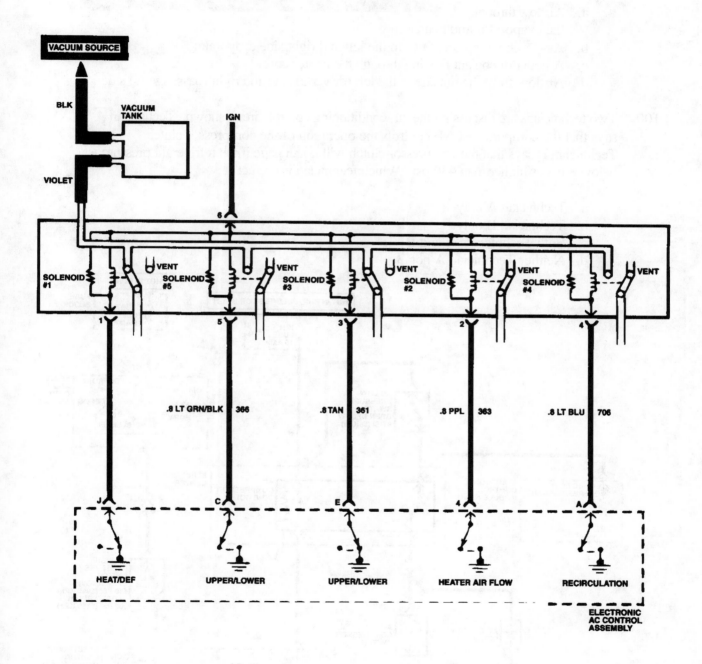

99. In the dual climate control system shown, the temperatures for the driver and passenger are regulated by controlling which components or system?

   a. Airflow through the evaporator and heater core
   b. Air-conditioning pressures to the left and right side evaporator
   c. Amount of coolant flowing through the heater core
   d. Airflow from the outside to the left (driver's) side and right (passenger's) side

100. Two technicians are discussing the air-conditioning control circuit shown. Technician A says that the computer (ECM) controls the operation of the compressor clutch. Technician B says that the compressor clutch will not engage if the refrigerant pressure is below 8 psi or higher than 430 psi. Which technician is correct?

   a. Technician A only
   b. Technician B only
   c. Both Technicians A and B
   d. Neither Technician A nor B

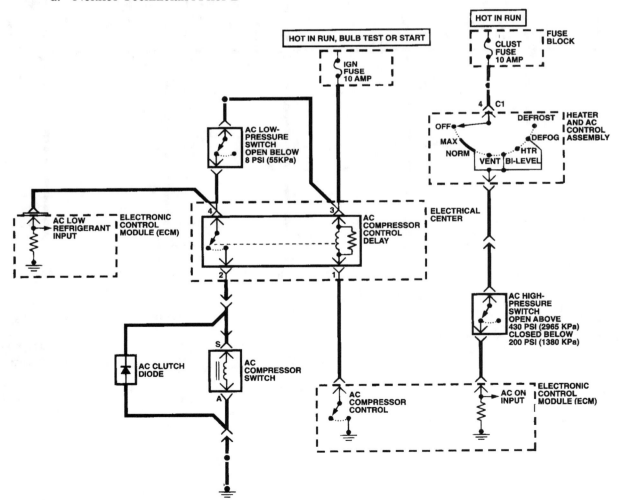

Heating and Air Conditioning (A7)

E. Refrigerant Recovery, Recycling, and Handling Questions

101.   The technician can test for trapped air (noncondensable gases) inside the refrigerant container by _____.

     a.   Checking the outside of the container for frost
     b.   Checking the pressure versus temperature of the container
     c.   Weighing the container
     d.   Sending the container to a special laboratory for analysis

102.   Technician A says that the refrigerant oil removed during reclaiming should be measured. Technician B says that refrigerant oil can be disposed of with regular engine oil. Which technician is correct?

     a.   Technician A only
     b.   Technician B only
     c.   Both Technicians A and B
     d.   Neither Technician A nor B

103.   Refrigerant should be identified _____.

     a.   After recovery, but before recycling
     b.   Before recovery
     c.   Before charging the system
     d.   After charging the system, but before releasing the vehicle to the customer

104.   To be sure that all of the moisture in an air-conditioning system has been boiled and removed, a vacuum of at least _____ in. Hg should be drawn on the system for at least _____ minutes.

     a.   28, 45
     b.   29, 60
     c.   30, 90
     d.   30, 120

105.   After the refrigerant has been recovered and recycled, where should it be kept for long-term storage?

     a.   In an EPA approved container
     b.   In the recovery machine storage unit
     c.   In the recycling machine storage unit
     d.   In a DOT approved container

106. What should the technician do before recovering refrigerant from a vehicle?

    a. Test it using a refrigerant identification machine
    b. Connect pressure gauges and check the high- and low-side pressures
    c. Tighten the Schrader valves to be sure they are properly sealed
    d. Start the engine and allow the air-conditioning system to work for several minutes

107. A technician discovers that 20% of the refrigerant in a vehicle is unknown. What service operation should the service technician perform?

    a. Recover and recycle the refrigerant as normal
    b. Recover the refrigerant into a container labeled unknown refrigerant
    c. Cycle the compressor clutch until the unknown refrigerant is purged from the system
    d. Recover the refrigerant and remove the noncondensable gases

108. A technician checked the pressure on a 30 lb. container of R-134a at 80°F (27°C) and the pressure was 101 psi (700 kPa) (see chart). Technician A says that the tank should be vented into a recovery machine until the pressure is reduced. Technician B says that additional refrigerant should be added to lower the pressure. Which technician is correct?

    a. Technician A only
    b. Technician B only
    c. Both Technicians A and B
    d. Neither Technician A nor B

| Maximum Container Pressure | | | | | |
| Temperature | | R-12 Pressure | | R-134a Pressure | |
°F	°C	psi	kPa	psi	kPa
70	21.1	80	552	76	524
75	23.9	87	600	83	572
80	26.7	96	662	91	627
85	29.5	102	703	100	690
90	32.2	110	758	109	752
95	35.0	118	814	118	814
100	37.8	127	876	129	889
105	40.6	136	938	139	958
110	43.4	146	1007	151	1041

109. According to the chart, how much vacuum needs to be applied to boil water from an air-conditioning system if the temperature is 78°F (26°C)?

    a. 0 in. Hg
    b. 15 in. Hg
    c. 29 in. Hg
    d. 30 in. Hg

BOILING POINT OF WATER UNDER VACUUM		
Vacuum Reading (in. Hg)	Pounds per Square Inch Absolute Pressure (psia)	Water Boiling Point°
0	14.696	212°F (100°C)
10.24	9.629	192°F (89°C)
22.05	3.865	151°F (66°C)
25.98	1.935	124°F (51°C)
27.95	0.968	101°F (38°C)
28.94	0.481	78°F (26°C)
29.53	0.192	52°F (11°C)
29.82	0.019	1°F (-17°C)
29.901	0.010	-11°F (-24°C)

110. An orifice tube-type air-conditioning system is being topped off using a small can (12 oz) of refrigerant. Technician A says that the system should be charged with the can in the upright position. Technician B says the system should be charged with the can in the inverted position. Which technician is correct?

    a. Technician A only
    b. Technician B only
    c. Both Technicians A and B
    d. Neither Technician A nor B

Heating and Air Conditioning (A7)

A. Air Condition System Diagnosis and Repair Answers and Explanations

1. **The correct answer is a.** Technician A only is correct because a system that is undercharged (low on refrigerant) will keep the compressor from creating pressure. As a result of the low amount of refrigerant, the cooling ability is reduced. Technician B is not correct because an inoperative cooling fan will cause the discharge pressure to increase rather than decrease because the air will not be forced through the condenser, thereby not allowing the heat to be transferred from the refrigerant to the outside air. Answers **c** and **d** are not correct because Technician A only is correct.

2. **The correct answer is a.** Technician A is correct because a cold blast from a CO_2 fire extinguisher onto the sensing bulb will cause the expansion valve to close if the sensing bulb and valve are working correctly. When the expansion valve closes, the low side pressure gauge reading will go into a vacuum indicating that the valve closed. Technician B is not correct because an orifice tube system does not use a temperature sensing bulb and would, therefore, be unaffected by the blast of a CO_2 fire extinguisher. Answers **c** and **d** are not correct because Technician A only is correct.

3. **The correct answer is d.** Neither technician is correct. Technician A is not correct because the line after the orifice tube should be cool indicating that the refrigerant has passed through a restriction and is expanding. The temperature also gets cooler as the refrigerant absorbs heat to change states from a liquid to a gas. Technician B is not correct because a clogged or partially clogged orifice tube would stop the flow of refrigerant causing the tube to be hot only on one side of the orifice tube. Answers **a, b,** and **c** are not correct because neither technician is correct.

4. **The correct answer is b.** Technician B only is correct because frost indicates that the component is cold and this can be caused if a restriction forces the high-pressure gas from the condenser to expand, thereby dropping the pressure and the temperature of the refrigerant as it flows through the restricted areas. Technician A is not correct because even though hot humid weather can contribute to frost formation, it is not normal for the section between the condenser and the receiver/drier to be cold. This section of the system should be warm because the refrigerant is a high-pressure liquid in this section. Answers **c** and **d** are not correct because Technician B only is correct.

5.   **The correct answer is a.** An insufficient amount of refrigerant metered into the evaporator will cause low pressure on both the low side gauge and the high side gauge and warmer than normal discharge air temperature. Answer **b** is not correct because a lack of airflow through the condenser will cause the high side pressure to be higher than normal. Answer **c** is not correct because while a defective compressor will cause a lower than normal high side pressure gauge reading, it will not cause the low side gauge to read lower than normal. Answer **d** is not correct because icing on the evaporator would be the result of a fault in the system that would allow the evaporator temperature to drop below freezing creating the ice, which would block the airflow.

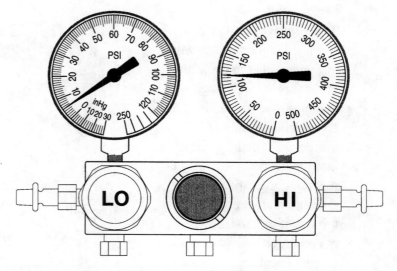

6.   **The correct answer is d.** An icing evaporator is the most likely cause to reduce the airflow and the heat load, which causes both low- and high-side pressures to be lower than normal. A fault in the temperature control is the most likely cause for the icing of the evaporator. Answer **a** is not correct because even though a low refrigerant level could cause both pressure gauges to read lower than normal, it would not cause the airflow to decrease after operating for a while. Answer **b** is not correct because even though a lack of airflow through the condenser would cause a lack of proper cooling, this condition would create an increase, rather than a decrease in high-pressure side and could not cause a decrease in airflow through the vents inside the vehicle. Answer **c** is not correct because even though a defective compressor could cause lower than normal pressure gauge readings, it could not cause a reduction in airflow through the vents.

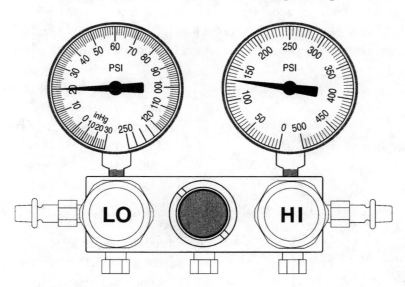

7. **The correct answer is b.** A restricted liquid line or a low refrigerant charge can cause this symptom and gauge readings, due to the fact that an inadequate amount of refrigerant is being metered into the evaporator. Answer **a** is not correct because the pressure gauge readings are too low if the system were overcharged. Answer **c** is not correct because the pressure gauge readings would be

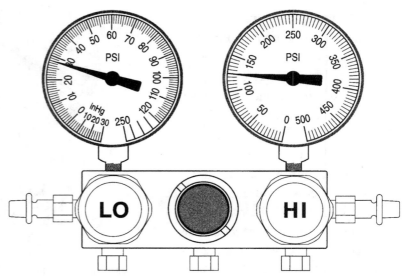

higher than normal, rather than lower than normal if there were a lack of proper airflow through the condenser. Answer **d** is not correct because a defective compressor would cause a higher than normal low-side pressure reading, not a reading that is lower than normal.

8. **The correct answer is c.** Excess refrigerant is the most likely cause for the higher than normal low-side pressure gauge reading. Too much refrigerant is being metered into the evaporator or the compressor is not pulling it out, which can occur on some systems that use a variable-displacement compressor. Answer **a** is not correct because a low refrigerant charge would cause the discharge air to be warm and both gauge pressure readings below normal. Answer **b** is not

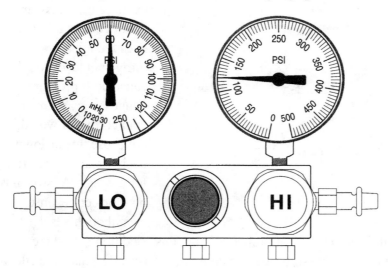

correct because a clogged condensate drain would cause water to overflow the evaporator housing and flow onto the floor of the vehicle and would not create higher than normal pressure on the low-side gauge. Answer **d** is not correct because a lack of airflow through the condenser would cause a higher than normal high-side pressure reading and not a higher than normal low-side pressure reading.

9. **The correct answer is d.** A clogged condenser coil or other obstruction that causes a lack of airflow through the condenser is the most likely cause of the warm discharge air temperature and the higher than normal pressures. Answer **a** is not correct because even though a system that is low on refrigerant will reduce cooling, the pressures would be lower, rather than higher than normal. Answer **b** is not correct because a defective compressor would cause the high-side pressure to be lower than normal, not higher than normal. Answer **c** is not correct because excess refrigerant would cause the discharge air temperature to be cool and a higher than normal low-side pressure and a normal high-side pressure rather than being above normal with a lack of cooling.

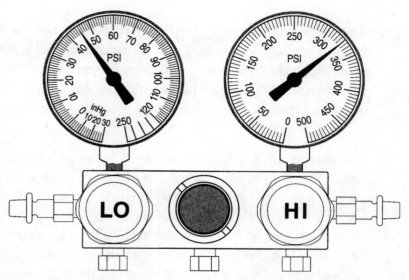

10. **The correct answer is a.** Technician A only is correct because a rapidly cycling compressor clutch is a common symptom of an air-conditioning system that is low on refrigerant. The compressor engages when the temperature (and pressure) rises, and then stops when the pressure is low. The low pressure is a result of a lack of refrigerant. Technician B is not correct because an electrical short would likely cause a fuse to blow and prevent the compressor clutch from operating entirely. Answers **c** and **d** are not correct because Technician A only is correct.

11. **The correct answer is a.** Technician A is correct because if the system is fully charged, the inlet of the evaporator, after the orifice tube, will be about the same temperature as the outlet of the evaporator. Technician B is not correct because the outlet temperature will be warmer than the inlet temperature if the system is low on refrigerant. Answers **c** and **d** are not correct because Technician A only is correct.

12. **The correct answer is c.** Both technicians are correct. Technician A is correct because if the system is partially charged (low on refrigerant), the cooling capacity is reduced and the system will not be able to properly cool the vehicle. Technician B is correct because if the cooling fan is not functioning, the condenser may not be able to dissipate the heat resulting in higher pressures and temperatures in the system and reduced cooling, especially in slow city-type driving conditions. Answers **a, b,** and **d** are not correct because both technicians are correct.

13. **The correct answer is b.** Technician B is correct because higher than normal pressures on both low-side and high-side gauges and warmer than normal vent discharge temperature is a symptom of air trapped in the system. Technician A is not correct because the pressure would be lower than normal, not higher than normal, if the system was low on refrigerant. Answers **c** and **d** are not correct because Technician B only is correct.

14. **The correct answer is a.** Technician A is correct because when the engine is off, the compressor stops and the high and low pressure in the system become equalized. This means that both the high-side pressure and the low-side pressure will be 70 psi at 70°F (21°C). Because the low-side increases (from normal of about 30 psi to 70 psi with the system off), it is more likely for leaks to be detected due to the higher pressure. Technician B is not correct because while the high side is best checked with the engine running and the system in operation, the low side is best checked with the engine off. Answers **c** and **d** are not correct because Technician A only is correct.

15. **The correct answer is b.** Technician B is correct because a partially blocked condenser will prevent air from removing the heat and create higher than normal high-side pressure. Technician A is not correct because a defective compressor is most likely to cause lower-than-normal high-side pressure due to its inability to compress the high temperature vapor. Answers **c** and **d** are not correct because Technician B only is correct.

16. **The correct answer is b.** Technician B is correct because when hot humid air comes in contact with the cooler evaporator coils, the moisture condenses into liquid water. This water flows out of the bottom of the evaporator housing through a small hole or opening and drips onto the ground. Technician A is not correct because if the evaporator were leaking, the refrigerant would vaporize and disappear as soon as it escaped from the sealed refrigerant system. Answers **c** and **d** are not correct because Technician B only is correct.

17. **The correct answer is b.** Technician B is correct because oil displaces refrigerant and even though the pressures are within the normal range, a lack of cooling will occur if excessive refrigerant oil has been installed in the system. Technician A is not correct because even though a partially clogged orifice tube will likely cause the lack of proper cooling, the high-side pressure will be lower than normal (not normal as stated) due to the lack of refrigerant flow through the compressor due to the restriction. Answers **c** and **d** are not correct because Technician B only is correct.

18. **The correct answer is a.** Technician A is correct because the orifice tube connects the low and high side pressure areas of the system. A partially clogged orifice tube is the most likely cause for a slow equalization of pressure after the engine stops. Technician B is not correct because a saturated desiccant will not cause the pressures to equalize slowly even though it could cause excessive moisture buildup to occur in the system leading to acid formation. Answers **c** and **d** are not correct because Technician A only is correct.

19. **The correct answer is b.** Water is created when warm moist air comes in contact with the cold evaporator. This water should drain out of the evaporator housing and fall onto the ground during normal air-conditioning operation unless the drain hole is clogged and the water overflows onto the floor on the passenger side of the vehicle. Answer **a** is not correct because an evaporator refrigerant leak would cause a discharged condition and the refrigerant would supply evaporate into the atmosphere and would not cause moisture to form on the carpet. Answer **c** is not correct because a saturated desiccant in the drier would allow moisture to build up inside the sealed system and would not cause water to form and drip onto the floor of the vehicle. Answer **d** is not correct because a clogged screen would reduce the flow of refrigerant within the system and could not cause water to drip onto the floor of the vehicle.

20. **The correct answer is a.** The gauge fittings must be unique to prevent the possibility of cross contamination between the two types of refrigerants and a label must be attached under the hood identifying the date and who did the retrofit. Answer **b** is not correct even though many manufacturers recommend that all of the O-rings be replaced. The compressor does not need to be replaced in most cases and therefore, it is not a required item. Answer **c** is not correct because even though the label must be installed, the condenser is not a required component that must be installed even though some vehicle manufacturers specify that it should be replaced. Answer **d** is not correct because the fittings must be replaced but the drier does not need to be replaced in all cases even though it is often recommended that it be replaced when retrofitting the system from R-12 to R-134a.

21. **The correct answer is d.** A disconnected vent tube is the most likely cause for the discharge air temperature to be greater in one vent. Answer **a** is not correct because too much refrigerant oil in the system would reduce the cooling for all vents and could not affect just the left side discharge vent temperature. Answer **b** is not correct because while a partially clogged orifice tube will cause a lack of cooling, it cannot cause a lack of cooling out of just one discharge air vent. Answer **c** is not correct because a blend door is used to adjust the amount of air that flows across the heater core after it has flowed through the evaporator to control the temperature of the discharge air and is not likely to cause a difference in air temperature at just one vent opening.

22. **The correct answer is c.** Both technicians are correct. Technician A is correct because the vehicle manufacturer must supply a label that identifies the type of refrigerant system and the recharge capacity. Technician B is correct because R-12 and R-134a pressure gauge fittings are unique. Answers **a, b,** and **d** are not correct because both technicians are correct.

23. **The correct answer is d.** A thermometer does not need to be placed in the recirculation door vent to perform an air-conditioning performance test because this would simply measure the temperature of the air being drawn back into the system to be cooled and would not be an important factor regarding the performance of the system. Answers **a, b,** and **c** are not correct because to perform an air-conditioning performance test, the blower should be on high (answer **a**), the doors should be open (answer **b**), and the controls set for maximum cooling (answer **c**).

24. **The correct answer is c.** Both technicians are correct. Technician A is correct because the oil specified by the vehicle manufacturer or the compressor manufacturer should be used to insure proper lubrication and this includes the specified type and viscosity of refrigerant oil. Technician B is correct because refrigerant oil readily absorbs moisture from the air and must be stored in an air-tight container to avoid moisture contamination. Answers **a, b,** and **d** are not correct because both technicians are correct.

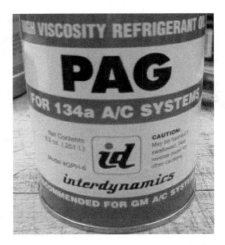

25. **The correct answer is c.** Both technicians are correct. Technician A is correct because debris from the old compressor can become trapped on the orifice tube causing a restriction limiting the flow of refrigerant into the evaporator. Technician B is correct because a leak would cause a lack of cooling due to less refrigerant flowing through the evaporator. Answers **a, b,** and **d** are not correct because both technicians are correct.

26. **The correct answer is a.** A disconnected vacuum hose is the most likely cause because the default position for the vacuum-controlled airflow doors is to the windshield and floor for safety reasons. Answer **b** is not correct because even though it may be possible for a defective mode control unit to cause this concern, it is not the most likely. Answer **c** is not correct because a discharged refrigerant system would cause a lack of cooling and would not cause the airflow to be directly to the windshield and floor. Answer **d** is not correct because a blend door is used to mix the air flowing through the evaporator through the heater core or bypass the heater core to control outlet temperature and is not used to direct the airflow to the windshield, floor, or dash vents.

27. **The correct answer is c.** Both technicians are correct. Technician A is correct because removing the blower motor resistor pack is a very efficient method to use to get access to the evaporator for leak detection. Technician B is correct because the condensate drain is located in the bottom of the evaporator housing and would provide access to the evaporator for leak detection. Answers **a, b,** and **d** are not correct because both technicians are correct.

28. **The correct answer is b.** A stuck idle air control (IAC) will not increase the idle speed necessary to keep the engine operating correctly when the load of the air-conditioning compressor is engaged. Answer **a** is not correct because a shorted engine coolant temperature (ECT) sensor would most likely trigger a diagnostic trouble code and may affect engine operation but not just when the air conditioning is engaged. Answer **c** is not correct because a clogged orifice tube would reduce the air-conditioning system effectiveness but would not affect the idle speed of the engine. Answers **d** is not correct because even though an overcharged air-conditioning system would cause a greater load to be placed on the engine, it is not as likely to cause an engine idle problem as answer **b**.

29. **The correct answer is d.** The least likely cause of a lack of cooling is a partially blocked condensate drain. A blocked condensate drain will cause an overflow of water of the evaporator case causing the floor of the passenger side to get wet but is unlikely to reduce cooling. Answers **a, b,** and **c** are not correct because all of these could cause reduced cooling.

30. **The correct answer is d.** Neither technician is correct. Technician A is not correct because the pressure displayed on the gauges indicates that the compressor is not engaged. The pressure of R-134a at 80°F (27°C) is about 87 psi indicating that the system has equalized and is not operating. Even though the system may have a partially clogged orifice tube, this cannot be determined by the pressure gauges because the compressor is not engaged. Technician B is not correct because even though the system may be undercharged, this condition cannot be determined because the compressor is not engaged. Answer **c** is not correct because neither technician is correct.

31. **The correct answer is c.** The most likely cause of a cool compressor and a higher than normal high-side pressure is an overcharge of refrigerant. A compressor should normally be warm to the touch. Answer **a** is not correct because a lack of oil in the system would tend to make the compressor operate hotter than normal rather than cool, due to the lack of lubrication. Answer **b** is not correct because an undercharged system results in lower than normal high-side pressures rather than higher than normal. Answer **d** is not correct because a restricted condenser would most likely cause the compressor to operate hotter than normal rather than cool to the touch.

32. **The correct answer is d.** Neither technician is correct. It is normal for the discharge line to be hot to the touch on a properly operating air-conditioning system. Technician A is not correct because a low charge would reduce the temperature of the discharge line. Technician B is not correct because a worn compressor would create less than normal heat and temperature of the discharge line. Answer **c** is not correct because neither technician is correct.

33. **The correct answer is b.** The most likely cause of bubbles (foam) in the sight glass is a low refrigerant charge. Answer **a** is not correct because nothing, or oil streaks, will be observed in the sight glass if the system is empty of refrigerant. Answer **c** is not correct because if the desiccant bags were ruptured, the sight glass will usually be clear when the system is properly charged or overcharged. Answer **d** is not correct because water is absorbed in the refrigerant and is not visible but will create acids, which will harm all components of the system.

34. **The correct answer is b.** Technician B is correct because a fungicide is necessary to kill fungus and mildew growth that can grow on the evaporator fins due to the moist environment. Technician A is not correct because even though most mouthwash contains alcohol, it will not be effective killing fungus and mildew. Answers **c** and **d** are not correct because Technician B only is correct.

Heating and Air Conditioning (A7)

B. Refrigeration System Component Diagnosis and Repair Answers and Explanations

35. **The correct answer is b.** Technician B is correct because refrigerant oil is hydroscopic and will absorb moisture from the air unless stored in a sealed container. Technician A is not correct because various types of refrigerant oils are used depending on the brand and type of compressor used in the system. Answers **c** and **d** are not correct because Technician B only is correct.

36. **The correct answer is b.** Defective engine mounts will allow the engine to move more than normal and place stress on the lines leading from the compressor, which is mounted on the engine, and on the condenser, which is mounted to the body. Answer **a** is not correct because shock absorbers would not affect the movement between the condenser, which is attached to the body, and the compressor, which is attached to the engine. Answer **c** is not correct because even though a defective cooling fan can reduce cooling, it would not cause excessive movement to occur in the line between the compressor and the condenser. Answer **d** is not correct because even though a defective compressor drive belt could cause a vibration, it would not cause movement between the compressor and the condenser.

37. **The correct answer is a.** Technician A is correct. The air gap must be correctly adjusted to allow clearance when the clutch is disengaged and proper holding power when the clutch is engaged. Technician B is not correct because even though the front seal could be replaced and may be leaking, it is not necessary to replace the front seal if the clutch is being replaced. Answers **c** and **d** are not correct because Technician A only is correct.

38. **The correct answer is b.** Technician B is correct. The air-conditioning compressor should engage when the HVAC control is set to defrost because the cool evaporator will cause moisture in the air to condense into liquid water before the air is directed to the windshield, thereby reducing the chances of fogging. Technician A is not correct because even though the air is directed through the evaporator, then through the heater core, very cold air is usually dry air and the compressor does not need to be operating to cool the evaporator when the heat position is selected. Answers **c** and **d** are not correct because Technician B only is correct.

39. **The correct answer is c.** Both technicians are correct. Technician A is correct because if the system were low on refrigerant charge, the system pressure would be low keeping the low pressure switch electrically open to prevent the operation of the compressor. This low pressure switch is designed to protect the compressor because if the system is low on charge, the refrigerant oil, needed by the compressor, will not be circulating through the system, which could cause compressor damage. Technician B is correct because the low pressure switch could be open electrically either due to a fault in the switch itself or due to the fact that the pressure in the system is not high enough to cause the switch to close. The low-pressure switch is usually connected in series with the compressor clutch and an open in the switch would prevent current from reaching and operating the compressor. Answers **a, b,** and **d** are not correct because both technicians are correct.

40. **The correct answer is c.** Both technicians are correct. Technician A is correct because a defective or excessively worn drive belt can cause noise that is often confused with a bearing noise. Technician B is correct because a defective compressor will often be noisy due to worn or damaged internal parts. Answers **a, b,** and **d** are not correct because both technicians are correct.

41. **The correct answer is b.** Technician B is correct. If oil is observed near the front of the compressor, the most likely cause is a small refrigerant leak from the front seal. While the refrigerant would immediately evaporate when it leaks from the seal, the oil that is mixed with refrigerant would condense and adhere to parts near the location of the leak. Technician A is not correct because even though the clutch is attached to the front of the compressor, it is the seal and not the clutch itself that prevents refrigerant leakage from occurring around the input shaft of the compressor. Answers **c** and **d** are not correct because Technician B only is correct.

42. **The correct answer is c.** Both technicians are correct. Technician A is correct because some refrigerant oil will remain in the old condenser. To ensure that the compressor gets enough lubrication, it is important that the correct amount of refrigerant oil be in the system. Most experts recommend that 1 ounce of oil be added to the system if the condenser is flushed or replaced. Technician B is correct because the wrong viscosity (thickness) of refrigerant oil could cause excessive wear and possible premature failure

of the compressor. Answers **a, b,** and **d** are not correct because both technicians are correct.

43. **The correct answer is d.** Neither technician is correct. Technician A is not correct because refrigerant oil contains traces of refrigerant and is considered to be hazardous if it contains chlorinated hydrocarbons. If this oil were to be mixed with engine oil, the entire quantity of oil has to be handled as hazardous waste. Technician B is not correct because only PAG or ester oil should be used in an R-134a system or damage to the compressor could result. Mineral oil does not mix with R-134a and would therefore not be circulated through the system. Answers **a, b,** and **c** are not correct because neither technician is correct.

44. **The correct answer is a.** Technician A is correct because the old evaporator has some refrigerant oil inside that cannot be drained but must be restored to ensure proper lubrication of the compressor. Most orifice tube system evaporators require 3 ounces of oil and most evaporators used on expansion valve systems require 2 ounces of oil be added to a new or flushed evaporator. Technician B is not correct because the amount of oil cannot be accurately measured if flushed or drained. Answers **c** and **d** are not correct because Technician A only is correct.

45. **The correct answer is b.** Technician B is correct because the inlet screen is designed to filter any debris that may clog the orifice tube and has a large surface area to help prevent it from restricting the flow of refrigerant. The shorter end of the tube faces the evaporator. Technician A is not correct because the inlet should face the condenser and not the evaporator. Answers **c** and **d** are not correct because Technician B only is correct.

46. **The correct answer is c.** Both technicians are correct. Technician A is correct because a lack of refrigerant oil can cause wear, which could lead to a noisy compressor. Technician B is correct because if the system is overcharged, some liquid refrigerant is likely to be drawn into the compressor causing noise because a liquid is not compressible. Serious damage to the reed valves and other compressor components is also possible. Answers **a, b,** and **d** are not correct because both technicians are correct.

47. **The correct answer is a.** A defective reed valve is the most likely fault because the valves would not seal properly causing the rapid oscillations in either or both manifold gauges. Answer **b** is not correct because a clogged orifice tube would restrict the flow of refrigerant and reduce cooling but is not likely to cause fluctuating pressure gauge readings. Answer **c** is not

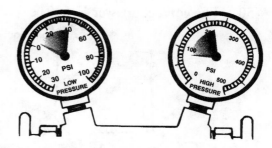

correct because an expansion valve that is stuck closed would prevent the flow of refrigerant through the system and the low side pressure will likely drop to zero or into a vacuum due to the action of the compressor. Answer **d** is not correct because if the desiccant bag were saturated with moisture, a buildup of acid could result, but it is unlikely to cause the pressure gauges to fluctuate.

48. **The correct answer is d.** The ohmmeter is measuring the resistance of the compressor clutch coil. Answer **a** is not correct because the meter is set to read resistance in ohms and not voltage. Answer **b** is not correct because the meter is set to read resistance in ohms and not voltage. Answer **c** is not correct because even though an ohmmeter could be used to check a radio suppression capacitor, it cannot be used to determine its capacitance.

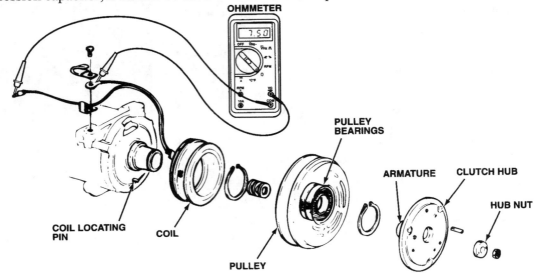

49. **The correct answer is b.** The tool being used is a puller and after the retaining nut and amp ring, if equipped, have been removed, the clutch assembly is pulled off of the compressor input shaft. Answer **a** is not correct because the puller is being used to remove, rather than install a component. Note that the jaws of the puller are gripping the housing of the compressor. Answer **c** is not correct because the tool is being used to remove the compressor clutch. Pulley alignment is achieved by shimming or correcting the compressor mount and not by adjusting the location of the drive pulley. Answer **d** is not correct because the drive pulley is one piece.

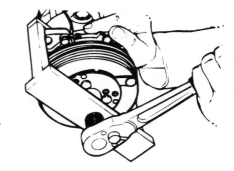

50. **The correct answer is d.** The special tool shown is being used to remove or install an orifice tube into the liquid line near the evaporator. Answers **a** and **b** are not correct because switches are not installed into the refrigerant line as shown but are accessible from the outside of the refrigerant lines using conventional tools. Answer **c** is not correct because even though the liquid line is being shown, the O-ring seal is installed on the outside rather than on the inside of the refrigerant line.

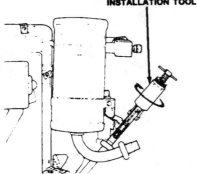

51. **The correct answer is c.** The special tool is used to release spring lock-type couplings used on some air-conditioning systems. Answers **a** and **b** are not correct because the tool is not needed to install O-rings. Answer **d** is not correct because an orifice tube is installed inside the liquid refrigerant line and is not on the outside of the line as shown.

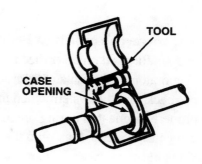

52. **The correct answer is a.** Technician A is correct because the compressor must have enough, but not too much, lubricating oil in the system. Because the compressor holds most of the oil in the system, it is important that the quantity be accurately measured so the correct amount can be installed in the system with the replacement compressor. Technician B is not correct because old refrigerant oil should not be reused. Most refrigerant oil is hydroscopic and absorbs moisture from the air, thereby becoming contaminated. Answers **c** and **d** are not correct because Technician A only is correct.

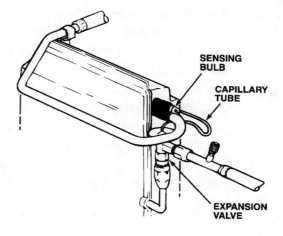

53. **The correct answer is a.** Technician A is correct because the capillary tube is part of the expansion valve and is serviced as an assembly. Technician B is not correct because the capillary tube is permanently attached and is part of the expansion valve and cannot be serviced separately. Answers **c** and **d** are not correct because Technician A only is correct.

54. **The correct answer is a.** Technician A is correct because the moisture in the air has caused the desiccant in the drier to become saturated and unable to provide further protection. Technician B is not correct because even though the refrigerant oil may have absorbed moisture during storage, the desiccant in the drier should be able to keep the formation of acid under control. Some vehicle manufacturers specify that the system should not be flushed because the flushing solvent remaining in the system may do more harm than if the system had not been flushed. Answers **c** and **d** are not correct because Technician A only is correct.

55. **The correct answer is c.** Both technicians are correct. Technician A is correct because an evaporator used on an orifice tube-type system typically holds 3 ounces of refrigerant oil and an evaporator used with an expansion valve holds about 2 ounces of oil. This amount of oil must be put back into the system when the evaporator is replaced to be sure that the compressor is properly lubricated during operation. Technician B is correct because a clogged condensate hole can cause water to leak onto the floor inside the vehicle or be picked up and sprayed from the AC vents in severe cases. Answers **a, b,** and **d** are not correct because both technicians are correct

56. **The correct answer is b.** Technician B is correct because a reading of 14.7 kΩ (14,700 ohms) means that the compressor clutch coil has extremely high resistance and will not function, requiring replacement. Technician A is not correct because the resistance measurement of the clutch coil is excessively high, which would cause a lack of current flow and an inoperative compressor clutch. Answers **c** and **d** are not correct because Technician B only is correct.

57. **The correct answer is d.** The amount of refrigerant oil in the compressor does not need to be checked if just the compressor clutch is being installed. Answers **a** (air gap), **b** (front seal leakage), and **c** (condition of the drive belt) are not correct because they all should be checked whenever replacing the compressor clutch assembly.

58. **The correct answer is a.** Technician A is correct because each application has a specified orifice tube size and improper cooling could result if an incorrect orifice tube were to be used. Technician B is not correct because the major difference in orifice tubes is not the outside diameter but the size of the orifice hole itself, which regulates the amount of refrigerant flow into the evaporator. Answers **c** and **d** are not correct because Technician A only is correct.

Heating and Air Conditioning (A7)

C. Heating and Engine Cooling Systems Diagnosis and Repair Answers and Explanations

59. **The correct answer is b.** Answer **b** is correct because if air is trapped in the heater core, the coolant cannot flow through and provide heat. This is a common problem because the heater core is usually located at the highest part of the cooling system and air always travels upwards. Answer **a** is not correct because even though the incorrect concentration of antifreeze in the coolant could affect the freezing protection and heat transfer ability of the coolant, it is unlikely to cause a lack of heat from the heater. Answer **c** is not correct because even though a defective heater control valve (stuck closed) could cause a lack of heat from the heater, it is unlikely to fail at the same time as the water pump repair and coolant replacement procedure. Answer **d** is not correct because even though a slipping water pump drive belt could reduce the flow of coolant through the system, it is unlikely to cause a lack of heat from the heater.

60. **The correct answer is b.** The most likely cause is a low coolant level causing coolant to flow through the heater core occasionally. Because the heater core is usually higher in the system than the engine block and the heater hoses create some resistance to coolant flow, most of the available coolant will flow through and protect the engine. Answer **a** is not correct because even though a defective thermostat could cause a lack of heat from the heater, it is unlikely to cause some heat at times and no heat at other times. Answer **c** is not correct because while a defective water pump could cause a lack of circulation, which could reduce the amount of heat from the heater, it is unlikely to cause the heat to come and go intermittently. Answer **d** is not correct because while an incorrect antifreeze to water mixture could cause corrosion or other cooling system related problems, it is unlikely to cause a lack of heat concern.

61. **The correct answer is a.** Technician A is correct because used coolant contains metals that were absorbed from the engine and cooling system components during engine operation and therefore, should be recycled by sending to an off-site recycling company or by doing it on-site using a coolant recycling machine. Technician B is not correct because most vehicle manufacturers advise against reusing coolant and usually specify that new coolant be used when refilling the cooling system. Answers **c** and **d** are not correct because Technician A only is correct.

62. **The correct answer is a.** Technician A is correct because the temperature of the coolant is regulated by the thermostat, and if it is stuck open or partially open, the coolant temperature will be lower than normal. Technician B is not correct because the fan helps remove heat from the radiator but does not regulate the coolant temperature. Answers **c** and **d** are not correct because Technician A only is correct.

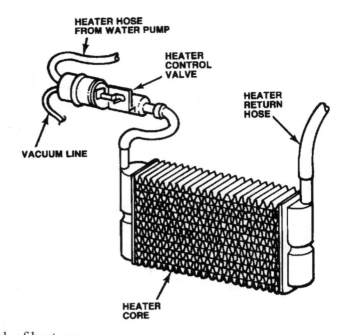

63.	**The correct answer is c.** The most likely cause of a lack of heat from the heater is a partially clogged heater core. Answer **a** is not correct because a clogged radiator would prevent the proper cooling of the coolant and would not cause a decrease in heater performance. Answer **b** is not correct because even though coolant flow could be affected slightly if the heater hoses were reversed, this condition would not prevent heat coming from the heater. Answer **d** is not correct because even though a defective water pump could reduce the flow of coolant through the system, it is not the most likely cause of a lack of heat concern.

64.	**The correct answer is d.** An inoperative cooling fan is the most likely cause of overheating at

slow speeds only because at highway speeds, normal airflow permits proper heat transfer from the radiator. Answer **a** is not correct because even though a low coolant level could cause overheating, it is not the most likely cause of overheating only when the vehicle is being driven at slow speeds. Answer **b** is not correct because even though an incorrect antifreeze/water mixture could cause cooling system problems, it is unlikely to cause overheating. Answer **c** is not correct because even though a defective water pump could cause overheating, it is unlikely to cause overheating only when the vehicle is being driven at slow speeds.

65.	**The correct answer is c.** Both technicians are correct. Technician A is correct because pure 100% antifreeze will freeze from -8°F to +8°F (-22°C to -13°C), unless it is mixed with water. Technician B is correct because too much water added to the coolant could raise the freezing point of the coolant. Answers **a, b,** and **d** are not correct because both technicians are correct.

66. **The correct answer is a**. Most vehicle manufacturers recommend that a 50/50 mix of antifreeze and water be used for the cooling system. Filling half the system with 100% antifreeze and the rest with water will result in a 50/50 mix. Answers **b** and **c** are incorrect because these methods will not result in a 50/50 antifreeze to water mix. Answer **d** will result in a 50/50 mix if all of the coolant can be drained from the system before refilling it with the 50/50 mix. However this method uses more antifreeze coolant than is necessary and therefore is not the recommended method and not the best answer to this question.

67. **The correct answer is d.** Neither technician is correct. Technician A is not correct because 210°F is within the normal operating range of a 195°F thermostat, which starts to open at 195°F and is fully open 20° higher or by 215°F. Technician B is not correct because even though a clogged radiator can cause the engine to overheat, the temperature of the coolant is within the normal range and a clogged radiator is not likely. Answers **a, b,** and **c** are not correct because neither technician is correct.

68. **The correct answer is c**. Both technicians are correct. Technician A is correct because the radiator should always be checked for proper operation before using it in a vehicle with a new or rebuilt engine. Technician B is correct because overheating during slow driving could be caused by an inoperative electric cooling fan. Answers **a, b,** and **d** are not correct because both technicians are correct.

69. **The correct answer is a**. Technician A is correct because the HOT light (engine coolant temperature warning lamp) will come on at about 258° F (125° C) to warn the driver that the engine coolant temperature is too high for safe engine operation. Technician B is not correct because the warning light does not react to cooling system pressure, just temperature. Answers **c** and **d** are not correct because only Technician A is correct.

70. **The correct answer is b.** Technician B is correct because the heater will have coolant flowing through the core when the water pump is operating slowly such as during engine idle. However, when the engine speed increases, the coolant will be taking the path of lower resistance and bypass the heater core unless the coolant level is properly filled. Technician A is not correct because even though the water pump could have worn impeller blades, the most likely cause is low coolant level. Answers **c** and **d** are not correct because only Technician B is correct.

71. **The correct answer is d**. Answer d is correct because normal operating temperature causes the upper hose to become hot and pressurized and will cause the cooling fans to cycle on and off. Answer **a** is not correct because the radiator cap will only release coolant to the overflow if the pressure exceeds the rating of the cap and does not represent what normally occurs when the engine reaches normal operating temperature. Answers **b** and **c** are not correct because either can be an indication of when normal operating temperature has been achieved and therefore, answer **d** is the best answer.

72. **The correct answer is b.** Technician B is correct because vehicle manufacturers specify a variety of coolants based on engine design as well as the materials used in the engine and cooling system. The specified coolant should be used to ensure proper service life. Technician A is not correct because even though conventional green antifreeze can provide the necessary cooling system protection against freezing, it may contain additives that are not compatible with the material used in the engine or cooling system. Answers **c** and **d** re not correct because Technician B only is correct.

73. **The correct answer is a.** A leaking heater core will cause the fogging of the windshield due to the pressure in the cooling system forcing the coolant through a hole in the heater core and through the ducts onto the windshield. Answer **b** is not correct because a leak in the evaporator would allow refrigerant to escape reducing the effectiveness of the air conditioning but will not cause the windshield to become fogged. Answer **c** is not correct because while a stuck blend door could affect the temperature of the discharge air 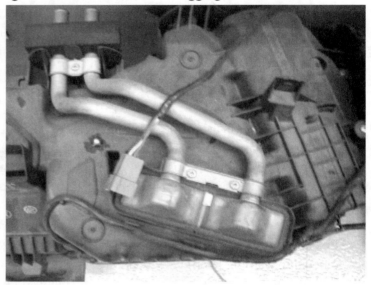 into the vehicle, it cannot cause fogging of the windshield. Answer **d** is not correct because if the air-conditioning system were low on refrigerant charge, the cooling of the interior would be reduced but would not cause the windshield to become fogged.

74. **The correct answer is c.** Both technicians are correct. Technician A is correct because the  system is obviously rusty and the system should be thoroughly flushed before being refilled with the proper coolant. Technician B is correct because the deposits cannot be thoroughly cleaned from the radiator cap and therefore, it should be replaced to ensure that the cap functions correctly. Answers **a, b,** and **d** are not correct because both technicians are correct.

75. **The correct answer is a.** A defective radiator cap would prevent the coolant from flowing back into the radiator as the engine cools and the coolant contracts creating a vacuum, which can cause the upper radiator to collapse. Answer **b** is not correct because even though the upper hose may be defective, it is not the cause of it collapsing as the engine cools. Answer **c** is not correct because even though a clogged radiator can cause

cooling system problems, it will not cause the upper radiator hose to collapse as the engine cools. Answer **d** is not correct because a low coolant level could cause overheating but not a collapsed upper radiator hose.

76. **The correct answer is c.** Both technicians are correct. Technician A is correct because the

leaking viscous silicone fluid is an indication that the unit may not be able to engage when the temperature rises high enough to require the additional airflow of the fan to properly cool the radiator. The wise technician should recommend that the unit be replaced before the engine overheats due to a lack of proper airflow through the radiator. Technician B is correct because the lack of airflow through the radiator can cause the engine to overheat especially during city driving. Answers **a, b,** and **d** are not correct because both technicians are correct.

77. **The correct answer is c.** Both technicians are correct. Technician A is correct because rust or

other contaminates could have caused the vanes of the pump to become corroded and flushing will clean the system to help prevent this type of reoccurring failure. Technician B is correct because some vehicle manufacturers recommend the use of antifreeze coolant that does not contain silicates that can lead to water pump wear as shown. Answers **a, b,** and **d** are not correct because both technicians are correct.

78. **The correct answer is b.** A leak in the evaporator would not cause the pressure in the cooling system to drop because it is part of the air-conditioning system and even though it is located in the same housing as the heater core, it is not part of the engine cooling system. Answers **a, c,** and **d** are not correct because a leak in any of these components would cause the pressure to drop in the cooling system.

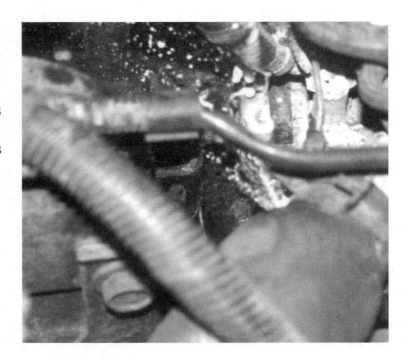

Heating and Air Conditioning (A7)

D. Operating System and Related Controls Diagnosis and Repair
Answers and Explanations

79.   **The correct answer is c.** Both technicians are correct. Technician A is correct because a power steering pressure sensor usually opens the electrical circuit to the compressor clutch when the power steering pressure rises above 300 psi (2000 kPa) indicating that the vehicle is turning and engine power is needed to drive the power steering pump. Technician B is correct because the low-pressure switch opens the electrical circuit to the compressor if the system pressure drops below a certain point that indicates the system is low on charge to help protect the compressor, which could fail due to lack of proper lubrication if allowed to operate with little if any refrigerant in the system. Answers **a, b,** and **d** are not correct because both technicians are correct.

80.   **The correct answer is b.** Technician B is correct because the default position for the mode door is the heat and defrost as a safety measure in the event of a failure. Technician A is not correct because the recirculation door simply opens the inlet to the inside or outside of the vehicle and would not affect where the air is directed. Answers **c** and **d** are not correct because Technician B only is correct.

81.   **The correct answer is a.** Technician A is correct because a defective compressor clutch clamping diode would cause the clutch to produce a high-voltage spike that will often cause the radio to pop through the speakers. Technician B is not correct because a poor ground connection would create excessive circuit resistance and would not cause the radio speakers to pop. Answers **c** and **d** are not correct because Technician A only is correct.

82.   **The correct answer is c.** Both technicians are correct. Technician A is correct because airflow would be restricted if dirt clogged the evaporator. The dirt usually will build up if there is a refrigerant leak, which also allows some refrigerant oil to escape. This oil coats the fins of the evaporator and traps dirt eventually restricting the airflow through the evaporator. Technician B is correct because if the blower motor ground had excessive resistance (high voltage drop), then current flow through the blower motor is reduced causing the fan to turn

slower than normal, which would reduce the airflow from the vents. Answers **a, b,** and **d** are not correct because both technicians are correct.

83.   **The correct answer is c.** Both technicians are correct. Technician A is correct because an open switch means that no current will flow through the switch to the compressor clutch circuit. Technician B is correct because a low-pressure switch is electrically open when the refrigerant pressure is too low to permit safe operation of the compressor. At low temperatures, the pressure of the refrigerant is often low enough to keep the low-pressure switch open, thereby preventing the operation of the compressor clutch. Answers **a, b,** and **d** are not correct because both technicians are correct.

84.   **The correct answer is c.** Both technicians are correct. Technician A is correct because many AC compressor clutches are disengaged when the accelerator pedal is depressed toward wide open throttle (WOT) either by a separate switch or by the computer responding to the signal from the throttle position (TP) sensor. Technician B is correct because many air-conditioning compressor clutches are disengaged by a power steering pressure switch when the power steering pressure rises above a certain level (usually about 300 psi (2000 kPa). Answers **a, b,** and **d** are not correct because both technicians are correct.

85.   **The correct answer is a.** Technician A is correct because if the inside air temperature sensor is blocked, the sensor will be unable to sense that cool air is being sent to the interior. As a result of this blocked sensor, the air-conditioning system will continue to deliver cool air waiting for the inside temperature sensor to react resulting in a cooler than normal temperature inside the vehicle. Technician B is not correct because if the sun load sensor were blocked, the temperature inside the vehicle would tend to be warmer than normal, not cooler than normal, because the system would not compensate for the heating effect of the sun inside the vehicle. Answers **c** and **d** are not correct because Technician A only is correct.

86. **The correct answer is a.** The resistance of engine coolant temperature (ECT) sensor is being measured because the sensor has been disconnected from power and the meter is set to read ohms. Answer **b** is not correct because the electrical connector is disconnected and the meter is not set to read voltage. Answer **c** is not correct because the electrical connector is disconnected and the meter is not set to read voltage. Answer **d** is not correct because the meter leads are touching the sensor wires and not the connector terminals.

87. **The correct answer is a.** Technician A is correct because the relay coil measures 70 ohms right in the middle of the usual reading of between 50 and 100 ohms for most relay coils. The OL reading between terminals #2 and #4 indicates that the relay contacts are open, which they should be until the coil is energized. Technician B is not correct because it is normal for the contacts to be open when the coil of the relay is not energized. Answers **c** and **d** are not correct because Technician A only is correct.

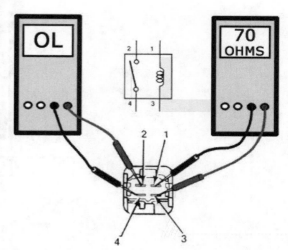

88. **The correct answer is c.** Both technicians are correct. Technician A is correct because even though the blower motor operates, it may be drawing more than the specified current. A fused jumper lead equipped with a 20 A fuse is a commonly used method to determine if the motor is drawing more than 20 A. Technician B is correct because an open in the fan control relay or resistor pack could cause the blower motor to not operate. Answers **a, b,** and **d** are not correct because both technicians are correct.

89. **The correct answer is d.** Neither technician is correct. Technician A is not correct because corroded ground connections would cause an increase in circuit resistance and a decrease (rather than an increase) in current flow through the motor. Technician B is not correct because a shorted blower relay would cause the blower motor to run all the time and would not cause the motor to draw more current as would occur if the motor itself were defective. Answer **c** is not correct because neither technician is correct.

90. **The correct answer is a.** Technician A is correct because an open high-pressure cutout switch would prevent the operation of the A/C compressor clutch. Technician B is not correct because the diode is used to reduce the voltage spike that occurs when the clutch is disengaged and would not prevent the clutch from engaging. Answers **c** and **d** are not correct because Technician A only is correct.

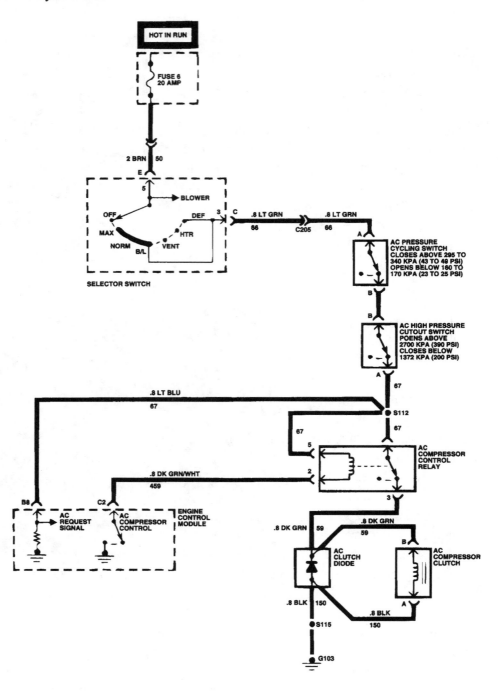

91. **The correct answer is b.** Worn or dry bearings will cause the motor to drag and operate at a slower than normal speed. Answer **a** is not correct because a blown resistor would cause an open circuit and prevent blower motor operation. Answer **c** is not correct because a bad switch could create a high resistance in the circuit but would more likely fail open thereby stopping the operation of the blower motor. Answer **d** is not correct because an open switch will stop the flow of electrical power to the motor and the motor would not operate.

92. **The correct answer is d.** Neither technician is correct. Technician A is not correct because an open thermal limiter would prevent the fan motor from operating at any speed and could not be the cause of the fan operating at low speed only. Technician B is not correct because an open at the "LO" contact in the switch would not affect the operation of the fan on the LO setting because no current flows through the switch when the low position is selected. Answers **a, b**, and **c** are not correct because neither technician is correct.

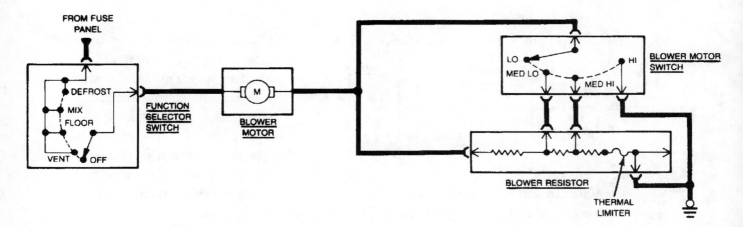

93. **The correct answer is d.** The ambient air temperature sensor is usually located in front of the radiator on most vehicles and if the sensor were damaged, it would prevent the operation of the air-conditioning compressor clutch. If the sensor is electrically open, the air-conditioning controller (computer) would interpret the sensor reading as being very cold and would prevent the operation of the compressor clutch. Answer **a** (reduced airflow through the radiator) is not correct because this condition could cause the engine to operate hotter than normal and could affect the

operation of the air conditioning, but is unlikely to prevent all cooling. Answer **b** is not correct because air trapped in the system, while it could reduce cooling, is unlikely to occur due to a collision. Answer **c** is not correct because even though a defective blower motor can cause a lack of proper interim cooling, it is unlikely to cause a total lack of cooling caused by a minor collision.

72

94. **The correct answer is c.** If the connector can loosen on the high-pressure switch, the electrical circuit would be broken and the compressor clutch would not engage as if the system pressure had reached an excessively high level. Answer **a** is not correct because the air conditioning would stop working and would not cause the temperature inside the vehicle to be cooler than normal. Answer **b** is not correct because even though the temperature will be warmer than normal, the most likely answer is that the air conditioning system will stop functioning. Answer **d** is not correct because the air-conditioning clutch would stop working entirely and would not cycle on and off.

95. **The correct answer is a.** Technician A is correct because the schematic shows a series circuit

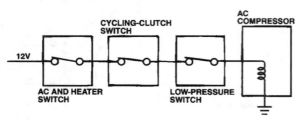

where all three switches must be closed to provide electrical power for the compressor clutch. Technician B is not correct because the low-pressure switch prevents the operation of the compressor clutch if the pressure drops to a low level and would therefore cause the low-pressure switch to open at low pressure, not close at low pressure. Answers **c** and **d** are not correct because Technician A only is correct.

96. **The correct answer is b.** The ohmmeter is used to check resistance and continuity (low resistance) through the wide-open throttle cutoff switch. The throttle cutoff switch opens the electrical circuit to the compressor clutch during wide-open throttle operating conditions to reduce the load on the engine so that maximum power can be applied to the drive wheels. Answer **a** is not correct because the meter is set to read ohms, not volts. Answer **c** is not correct because the meter is set to read resistance (ohms) and is not set to measure current flow (amperes). Answer **d** is not correct because the drawing shows the wide-open throttle cutoff switch and not the compressor clutch coil.

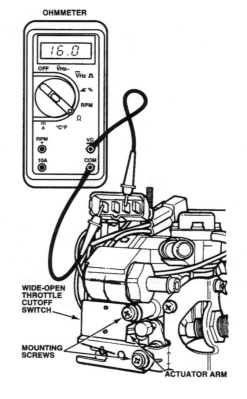

97. **The correct answer is c.** Both technicians are correct. Technician A is correct because a fault in the HVAC control head could prevent the grounding (operation) of the vacuum control solenoids. Technician B is correct because the fault in the defroster solenoid would prevent the proper flow of air to the windshield and could prevent defroster operation. Answers **a, b,** and **d** are not correct because both technicians are correct.

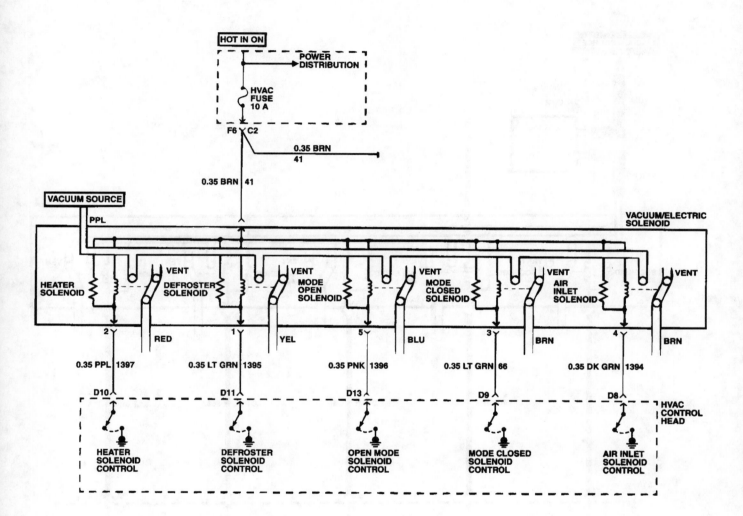

98. **The correct answer is d.** The electronic AC control assembly controls the ground side of the vacuum control solenoids and the "heat/def" solenoid and the "upper/lower" solenoid are grounded indicating that the airflow is to the windshield (defrost) and heat (floor) positions. Answers **a, b,** and **c** are not correct because the vacuum is directed to the vent and is not applied to the actuators, which direct the airflow.

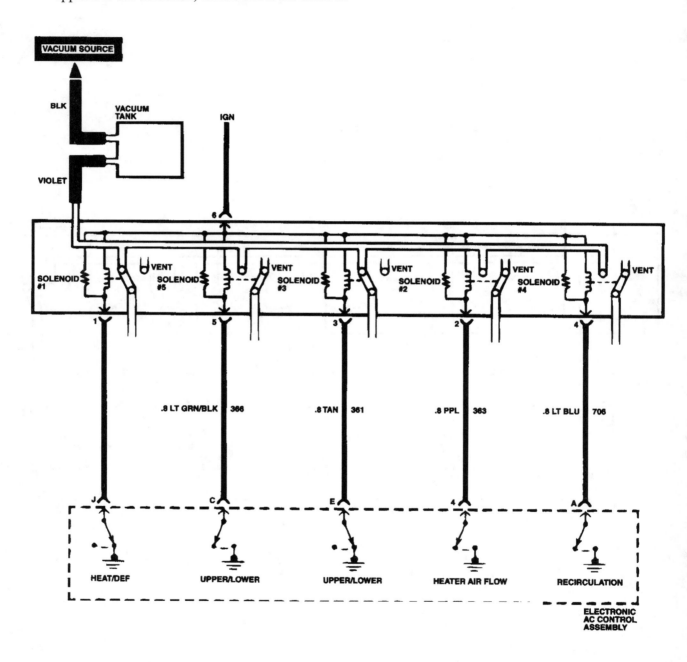

99. **The correct answer is a.** The temperature of air directed to the driver side and passenger side is regulated by controlling the airflow through the evaporator (to cool and dehumidify the air), then through the heater core (if needed) to warm the air before being sent to the discharge vents. Answer **b** is not correct because even though some rear air-conditioning systems used in vans or SUVs use two evaporators, most dual-climate control systems use just one evaporator and control the airflow through the system to deliver different temperatures for the driver and passenger sides of the vehicle. Answer **c** is not correct because the amount of coolant flowing through the heater core is constant except during maximum cooling mode. Answer **d** is not correct because even though the system does use outside air, it is then passed through the evaporator and heater core to achieve the desired temperature rather than just using outside air to control the temperature.

100. **The correct answer is c.** Both technicians are correct. Technician A is correct because the actual electrical connection to ground for the compressor clutch coil relay is inside the computer. When the relay coil is grounded by the computer, the relay coil is energized and current flows from the ignition fuse through the relay contacts to the compressor clutch. Technician B is correct because the compressor clutch coil circuit opens if either the low-pressure switch or the high-pressure switch opens. Answers **a, b,** and **d** are not correct because both technicians are correct.

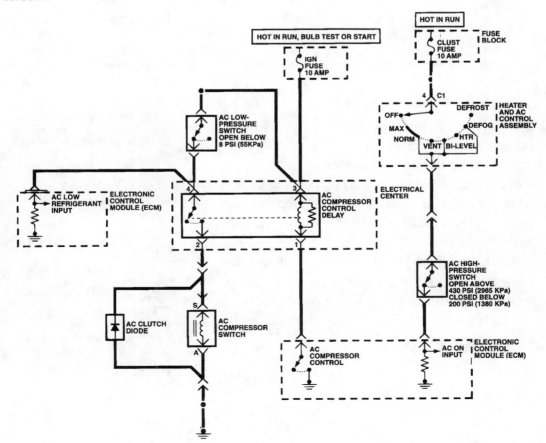

Heating and Air Conditioning (A7)

E. Refrigerant Recovery, Recycling, and Handling
Answers and Explanations

101. **The correct answer is b.** Air is a noncondensable gas and adds pressure to the container yet it does not contribute to the cooling capacity of the refrigerant. If the pressure is higher, as shown on the chart, it contains noncondensable gases. Answer **a** is not correct because frost on the container is an indication that refrigerant is leaving the container causing the pressure and temperature to drop, and not an indication of the presence of air (noncondensable gases). Answer **c** is not correct because the weight will not indicate the pressure of air, just the amount of refrigerant that is in the container. Answer **d** is not correct because air can be detected by comparing the pressure inside the container to a chart, which shows what the pressure should be for a container of a certain temperature. If the pressure is higher than the chart indicates, noncondensable gases are present in the container.

Maximum Container Pressure					
Temperature		R-12 Pressure		R-134a Pressure	
°F	°C	psi	kPa	psi	kPa
70	21.1	80	552	76	524
75	23.9	87	600	83	572
80	26.7	96	662	91	627
85	29.5	102	703	100	690
90	32.2	110	758	109	752
95	35.0	118	814	118	814
100	37.8	127	876	129	889
105	40.6	136	938	139	958
110	43.4	146	1007	151	1041

102. **The correct answer is a.** Technician A is correct because any refrigerant oil that is removed from the system during the recovery process must be measured to be assured that the proper amount of oil is in the system when recharged. Technician B is not correct because the refrigerant oil might contain hydrofluorocarbons (R-134a) or chlorofluorocarbons (R-12) making the oil hazardous and unable to be recycled as conventional waste oil. Answers **c** and **d** are not correct because Technician A only is correct.

103. **The correct answer is b.** The refrigerant should be identified before it is recovered to guard against the possibility of contaminating the storage container or the recovery/recycling equipment with an unknown refrigerant. Answers **a, c,** and **d** are not correct because the refrigerant should be checked before any service work is performed on the system.

104. **The correct answer is a.** The refrigerant system should be evacuated to a level of 28 in. Hg or higher, for at least 45 minutes to be sure that the moisture is boiled out of the system. Answers **b, c,** and **d** are all possible and should be done, but the question asks what values are the minimum that should be achieved to be sure that the moisture is boiled out of the system before recharging with refrigerant.

105. **The correct answer is d.** Refrigerant should be stored in a container that meets Department of Transportation (DOT) standards because it will be transported. Answer **a** is not correct because the container has to meet DOT, not EPA standards to be able to be shipped. Answers **b** and **c** are not correct because even though refrigerant can be kept in the recovery or recycling machine, eventually it must be transferred to another storage container.

106. **The correct answer is a.** Before refrigerant is recovered, a refrigerant identification machine should be used to avoid the possibility that the system has the wrong refrigerant or a mixture of refrigerants. Answer **b** is not correct because the wrong refrigerant could be exposed to the pressure gauges and/or equipment used to check high and low pressures. Answer **c** is not correct because even though the Schrader valves should be checked, it is not the first item that should be done before recovering refrigerant. Answer **d** is not correct because even though starting the engine and allowing the system to operate for a few minutes will not do any harm, it is not a necessary first step before refrigerant recovery.

107. **The correct answer is b.** The best answer is to recover the refrigerant into a separate container labeled unknown and to dispose of the contents of the container when full through a licensed recycler. Answer **a** is not correct because the unknown refrigerant can contaminate the recovery/recycling equipment. Answer **c** is not correct because the unknown refrigerant will not be or should not be purged from the system. Answer **d** is not correct because unknown refrigerant is not the same as noncondensable gases (air).

108. **The correct answer is a.** Technician A is correct because according to the chart, the container pressure should not exceed 91 psi (627 kPa) unless there is some air in the tank which contributes to the pressure but does not act as a refrigerant. The tank should be vented into a recovery machine until the pressure is restored to normal. Technician B is not correct because additional refrigerant would not reduce the pressure in the storage container. Answers **c** and **d** are not correct because Technician A only is correct.

Maximum Container Pressure					
Temperature		R-12 Pressure		R-134a Pressure	
°F	°C	psi	kPa	psi	kPa
70	21.1	80	552	76	524
75	23.9	87	600	83	572
80	26.7	96	662	91	627
85	29.5	102	703	100	690
90	32.2	110	758	109	752
95	35.0	118	814	118	814
100	37.8	127	876	129	889
105	40.6	136	938	139	958
110	43.4	146	1007	151	1041

109. **The correct answer is c.** According to the chart, a vacuum of at least 29 in. Hg is necessary to boil water from the air-conditioning system at a temperature of 78°F (26°C). Answers **a** and **b** are not correct because the levels of vacuum will not be low enough to cause any trapped moisture in the system to boil. Answer **d** is not correct because even though 30 in. Hg will cause any moisture in the system to boil, it is not the minimum vacuum that is necessary to boil moisture out of the system.

BOILING POINT OF WATER UNDER VACUUM		
Vacuum Reading (in. Hg)	Pounds per Square Inch Absolute Pressure (psia)	Water Boiling Point°
0	14.696	212°F (100°C)
10.24	9.629	192°F (89°C)
22.05	3.865	151°F (66°C)
25.98	1.935	124°F (51°C)
27.95	0.968	101°F (38°C)
28.94	0.481	78°F (26°C)
29.53	0.192	52°F (11°C)
29.82	0.019	1°F (-17°C)
29.901	0.010	-11°F (-24°C)

110. **The correct answer is c.** Both technicians are correct. Technician A is correct because with the can in the upright position, vapor only will be drawn into the system, which will not cause harm to the system. Technician B is correct because with an orifice tube-type system, the refrigerant can be added in liquid form (can inverted) because it is flowing into the accumulator and is unlikely to cause compressor damage as could occur if liquid were installed on the low side near the compressor. Answers **a, b,** and **d** are not correct because both technicians are correct.

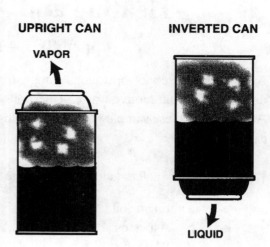

Heating and Air Conditioning (A7)

Appendix 1 – Environmental Questions

All automotive service operations assume that the service technician will adhere to proper handling and disposal of all automotive waste. Questions about environmental issues are not asked on the actual ASE test, but these sample questions will test your knowledge of the proper ways to handle these issues.

1. Hazardous materials include all of the following except _____.

   a. Engine oil
   b. Asbestos
   c. Water
   d. Brake cleaner

2. To determine if a product or substance being used is hazardous, consult _____.

   a. A dictionary
   b. A MSDS
   c. SAE standards
   d. EPA guidelines

3. Technician A says that used engine oil can be used in waste oil heaters. Technician B says that waste oil can be recycled by a licensed recycler. Which technician is correct?

   a. Technician A only
   b. Technician B only
   c. Both Technicians A and B
   d. Neither Technician A nor B

4. Two technicians are discussing what to do with used antifreeze coolant. Technician A says that it can be recycled either onsite or offsite. Technician B says that it can be poured down the drain. Which technician is correct?

   a. Technician A only
   b. Technician B only
   c. Both Technicians A and B
   d. Neither Technician A nor B

5. Used antifreeze coolant is often considered hazardous waste because it contains _____.

   a. Ethyl glycol
   b. Water (H_2O)
   c. Dissolved metal(s)
   d. Organic acids

6. Two technicians are discussing corrosive materials. Technician A says that a substance with a pH of 2 or lower is a strong acid. Technician B says that a substance with a pH of 12.5 or higher is caustic. Which technician is correct?

   a. Technician A only
   b. Technician B only
   c. Both Technicians A and B
   d. Neither Technician A nor B

7. Two technicians are discussing material safety data sheets (MSDS). Technician A says to look for the ingredients that contain the letters "clor" or "fluor". Technician B says to look for a flash point below 140°F (60°C). Which technician is correct?

   a. Technician A only
   b. Technician B only
   c. Both Technicians A and B
   d. Neither Technician A nor B

8. Two technicians are discussing used batteries. Technician A says that they should be considered hazardous waste and should be recycled by a licensed recycler. Technician B says to store used batteries near a drain in case they leak acid. Which technician is correct?

   a. Technician A only
   b. Technician B only
   c. Both Technicians A and B
   d. Neither Technician A nor B

9. Technician A says that gasoline should always be stored in red containers. Technician B says that gasoline should always be stored in sealed containers. Which technician is correct?

   a. Technician A only
   b. Technician B only
   c. Both Technicians A and B
   d. Neither Technician A nor B

10. Hazardous waste should be handled by the shop or repair facility and records kept of which of the following:

    a. Name of the company or individual that disposes of the waste
    b. Where it is being sent
    c. What is going to happen to the waste
    d. All of the above

Heating and Air Conditioning (A7)

Appendix 1 – Environmental Answers

1.   **The correct answer is c.** Water is not considered to be a hazardous material unless it is contaminated by other elements that are considered to be hazardous. Answer **c** is not correct because engine oil is considered to be hazardous because of the dissolved metals and accumulated acid that used oil contains. Answer **b** is not correct because asbestos is considered to be a cancer causing material if breathed. Answer **d** is not correct because brake cleaner often contains solvents or other volatile organic compounds (VOL) that are considered to be hazardous.

2.   **The correct answer is b.** The material safety data sheet (MSDS) is the best source for information regarding a product or substance. Answer **a** is not correct because a product or substance is often a combination of ingredients and would not be listed or described in a dictionary. Answers **c** and **d** are not correct because even though these organizations have established standards, the product or substance could meet these standards and still be considered hazardous.

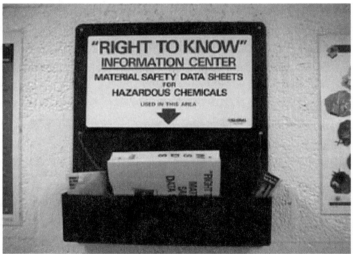

3.   **The correct answer is c.** Technician A is correct because waste oil can be burned in a waste oil heater with a capacity of less than 500,000 BTUs. Technician B is correct because used (waste) oil can be recycled by a licensed recycler. Answers **a**, **b**, and **d** are not correct because both technicians are correct.

4.   **The correct answer is a.** Used antifreeze coolant can be recycled either on site or shipped to a licensed recycler off site. Technician B is not correct because unless a permit is applied for and granted, it is generally not acceptable to pour used coolant down a sanitary sewer. Answers **c** and **d** are not correct because only Technician A is correct.

5. **The correct answer is c.** Antifreeze coolant (ethylene glycol) by itself is not considered to be hazardous. When the coolant is used in an engine, it can absorb metals such as iron, steel, copper, and lead from the cooling system components, which can cause the coolant to become hazardous. Answer **a** is not correct because most coolant is mostly ethylene glycol with about 5% additives and by itself is not considered to be hazardous. Answer **b** is not correct because even though water containing chemicals can be considered to be hazardous, water by itself is not hazardous. Answer **d** is not correct because the acid content would have to be high enough to lower the pH form about 7-12 down to 2 or less to be considered hazardous.

6. **The correct answer is c.** Technician A is correct because a pH of 2 or less is considered to be strong acid and is very corrosive. Technician B is correct because any substance with a pH of 12.5 or higher is very caustic and is considered to be hazardous. Answers **a**, **b**, and **d** are not correct because both technicians are correct.

7. **The correct answer is c.** Technician A is correct because most hazardous materials contain chemicals that have the letter "clor" or "fluor" in their ingredients as described in the material safety data sheet (MSDS). Technician B is correct because a material is considered to be hazardous if it has a flash point (temperature where it will ignite) below 140°F (60°C). Gasoline is an example of a product that has a flash temperature below 140°F. Answers **a**, **b**, and **d** are not correct because both technicians are correct.

8. **The correct answer is a.** Used batteries should be recycled and transported to an EPA approved recycling facility. Answer **b** is not correct because batteries should be stored away from drains to prevent the possibility that battery acid could seep into the sanitary or storm sewer. Answers **c** and **d** are not correct because only Technician A is correct.

9. **The correct answer is c.** Technician A is correct because gasoline should only be stored in red containers for easy identification. Technician B is correct because gasoline should always be stored in a sealed container to prevent the escape of gasoline fumes, which could be easily ignited. Answers **a**, **b**, and **d** are not correct because both technicians are correct.

10. **The correct answer is d.** A shop handling hazardous waste must keep records which include **a** the name of the company or individual that disposes of the waste, **b** the location where the material is sent, and **c** how the waste is going to be disposed of when it reaches the site. Answers **a**, **b**, and **c** are not correct because all three answers are correct.

Heating and Air Conditioning (A7)

Appendix 2 – Safety Questions

All automotive service operations assume that the service technician will practice safe work habits. Questions about safety issues are not asked on the actual ASE test, but these sample questions will test your knowledge of the proper ways to handle these issues.

1.   All equipment used in the shop must be designed to meet what safety standards?

       a. Occupational Safety and Health Act (OSHA)
       b. Environmental Protection Agency (EPA)
       c. Resource Conservation and Recovery Act (RCRA)
       d. Workplace Hazardous Material Information Systems (WHMIS)

2.   All items are considered to be personal protection equipment (PPE) **except**:

       a. Safety glasses
       b. Gloves
       c. Hearing protection
       d. Hair net

3.   When should service technicians wear ear protection?

       a. If the sound level is high enough that you must raise your voice to be heard
       b. Above 90 dB (a lawnmower is about 110 dB)
       c. When using a torch
       d. Both a and b

4.   A service technician should _____.

       a. Pull on a wrench
       b. Push on a wrench
       c. Use your legs when lifting heavy loads
       d. Both a and c

5.   A three-prong 110-volt plug is being used, but it will not fit the two-prong outlet. What should the technician do?

       a. Cut off the round ground prong
       b. Use an adapter from the three-prong plug to the two-prong electrical outlet
       c. Attach a grounded adapter and connect the green ground wire to the outlet housing before using the electrical device
       d. Use a cordless tool

6.   Personal protection equipment (PPE) can include _____.

    a.   Steel-toe shoes
    b.   Face mask
    c.   Gloves
    d.   All of the above

7.   The shop should have _____.

    a.   Guards in good condition installed on machinery
    b.   Shop/bay floors that are clean and dry
    c.   Fire extinguishers that are properly charged and easily accessible
    d.   All of the above

8.   What type of fire extinguisher should be used to put out an oil or grease fire?

    a.   Water
    b. CO_2
    c.   Dry chemical
    d.   Either b or c

9.   To what does the term "lockout" or LO/TO refer?

    a.   A union strike
    b.   A lock placed on the lever that disconnects electrical power
    c.   A type of hand tool
    d.   A safety ground fault switch

10.   A service technician should wear personal protection equipment to be protected against all **except** _____.

    a.   Used oil
    b.   Pumice-type cleaners
    c.   Falling heavy objects
    d.   Loud noises

Heating and Air Conditioning (A7)

Appendix 2 – Safety Question Answers

1. **The correct answer is a.** Shop equipment must meet the standards established by the Occupational Safety and Health Act (OSHA). Answers **b**, **c**, and **d** are not correct because the EPA, RCRA, and WHMIS regulate air, water, ground contamination, and hazardous materials and are not associated with the specifications of shop equipment.

2. **The correct answer is d.** Answer **d** is correct; a hair net is used to prevent hair from falling into food and is not generally considered to be safety equipment, even though long hair could get caught in machinery. Answers **a**, **b**, and **c** are all considered to be personal protection equipment.

3. **The correct answer is d.** Answer **a** is correct because ear protection should be worn if the surrounding noise level is high enough that it requires you to raise your voice to be heard. Answer **b** is correct because the OSHA standard requires that ear protection be used whenever noise levels exceed 90 dB. Answer **c** is not correct because a torch will usually not create noise above 90 dB.

4. **The correct answer is d.** Answer **a** is correct because a technician should pull (instead of push) a wrench. Answer **c** is correct because a technician should use his/her legs and not his/her back to lift heavy objects. Answer **b** is not correct because a technician could be injured by pushing on a wrench when the fastener breaks loose or if the wrench slips.

5. **The correct answer is c.** Answer **c** is correct because a three-prong plug to a two-prong electrical outlet adapter has a green wire pigtail that should be attached to the outlet box to be assured that the device is properly grounded. Answer **a** is not correct because if the ground prong is cut off, the device has no electrical path to ground and could create a shock hazard. Answer **b** is not correct because simply using an adapter without grounding the adapter prevents the device from being properly grounded, which could cause a shock hazard. Answer **d** is not correct because even though a cordless tool would not create a hazard, the question states that a three-prong plug is being used and the best answer is **c**.

6. **The correct answer is d.** Answers **a**, **b**, and **c** are correct because steel-toe shoes, face mask, Appendix 2 Safety.docand gloves are all considered to be personal protection equipment (PPE). Answers **a**, **b**, and **c** are not correct because all three items are considered to be PPE, not just one of the items.

7.   **The correct answer is d.** Answer **a** is correct because guards must be installed on all machinery that requires a guard and they must be in good condition. Answer **b** is correct because the shop/bay floors should be clean and dry to prevent slippage, which could cause personal injury. Answer **c** is correct because fire extinguishers must be fully charged and easily accessible. Answers **a**, **b**, and **c** are not correct because all three items should be present in all shops.

8.   **The correct answer is d.** Answer **b** is correct because a CO_2 fire extinguisher can be used on almost any type of fire including an oil or grease fire. Answer **c** is correct because a dry chemical fire extinguisher can also be used on most types of fires including an oil and grease fire. Answer **a** is not correct because water is heavier than oil and will cause the oil to float on the surface of the water.

9.   **The correct answer is b.** Answer **b** is correct because the term lock out/try out (LO/TO) refers to physically installing a lock on the electrical box that would prevent the accidental switching on of electrical power to the circuit being serviced. Answer **a** is not correct because even though the term lockout is used to describe some actions, the term LO/TO is used mostly to describe the locking out of an electrical circuit. Answers **c** and **d** are not correct because they do not describe the locking out of electrical power.

10.   **The correct answer is b.** Answer **b** is correct because pumice-type cleaners are typically used to wash hands and are not considered to be hazardous. Answers **a**, **c**, and **d** are not correct because the question asks which is not a possible hazardous material.

A7 English-Language Glossary

Accumulator – A component that is located between the evaporator and the compressor on the low side of the system. This unit stores excess refrigerant vapor in an air-conditioning system that uses an orifice tube.

Align - To bring the parts of a unit into the correct position.

Alloy - A metal that contains one or more other elements usually added to increase strength or give the base metal important properties.

Alternator - An electric generator that produces alternating current but is rectified to DC current by diodes. Also called an *AC generator*.

Altitude - Elevation as measured in relationship to the earth's surface at sea level.

Ambient air temperature - The temperature of the air surrounding an object.

Ammeter - An electrical test instrument used to measure amperes (unit of the amount of current flow).

Ampere - The unit of the amount of current flow. Named for André Ampère (1775–1836).

Amplitude - The difference between the highest and lowest level of a waveform.

Analog - A type of dash instrument that indicates values by use of the movement of a needle or similar device. An analog signal is continuous and variable.

Anode - The positive electrode; the electrode toward which electrons flow.

ANSI - American National Standards Institute.

API - American Petroleum Institute.

APRA - Automotive Parts Rebuilders Association.

ASE - Abbreviation for the National Institute for Automotive Service Excellence, a nonprofit organization for the testing and certification of vehicle service technicians.

ASTM - American Society for Testing Materials.

Atmospheric pressure - Pressure exerted by the atmosphere on all things based on the weight of the air.

Atom - An atom is the smallest unit of matter that still retains its separate unique characteristics.

Atomize - To reduce or separate into fine or minute particles.

AWG - American Wire Gauge system.

Baffle - A plate or shield used to direct the flow of a liquid or gas.

Bakelite - A brand name of the Union Carbide Company for phenolformaldehyde resin plastic.

Barometric pressure - The measure of atmospheric pressure, in inches of mercury (Hg), that reflects altitude and weather conditions.

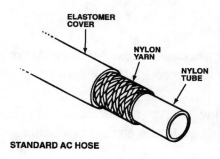

STANDARD AC HOSE

Barrier hose - A type of air-conditioning hose that includes a barrier layer on the inside to help prevent the loss of refrigerant through the hose. Barrier hoses are usually required for use with HFC-134a refrigerant.

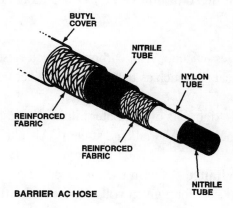

BARRIER AC HOSE

Base - The name for the section of a transistor that controls the current flow through the transistor.

Battery - A chemical device that produces a voltage from two dissimilar metals submerged in an electrolyte.

Baud rate - The speed at which bits of computer information are transmitted in a serial data stream; measured in bits per second (bps).

Bidirectional communication - Computer communication that uses serial data as both an input and an output.

Bit - The individual voltage signal of a serial data stream; also, the smallest unit of measurement recognized by a computer.

Blower-motor - An electric motor and squirrel-cage type of fan that moves air inside the vehicle for heating, cooling, and defrosting.

BNC connector - Coaxial-type connector usually used on oscilloscopes. Named for its inventor, Baby Neil Councilman.

Brinelling - A type of mechanical failure used to describe a dent in metal such as what occurs when a shock load is applied to a bearing. Named after Johann A. Brinell, a Swedish engineer.

British thermal unit (BTU) - The amount of heat required to raise 1 pound of water 1° F at sea level.

Brushes - A copper or carbon conductor used to transfer electrical current from or to a revolving electrical part such as that used in an electrical motor or generator.

Byte - Eight bits of computer information that are processed as a unit and are transmitted in sequence on the serial data stream. Also known as a *word*.

Capacitance - A term used to measure or describe how much charge can be stored in a capacitor (condenser) for a given voltage potential difference. Capacitance is measured in farads or smaller increments of farads such as microfarads.

Capacitor - Also called a *condenser*. An electrical unit that can pass alternating current yet block direct current; used in electrical circuits to control fluctuations in voltage.

CCOT - An abbreviation often used to identify an air-conditioning system that uses a cycling clutch orifice tube.

Centi-Stoke – (cSt); centimeter per gram per second; unit of measure of viscosity.

CFC-12 - Air conditioning refrigerant, also called R-12, whose chemical name is diclorodifluoromethane.

Chassis - The frame, suspension, steering and machinery of a motor vehicle.

Chassis ground - In electrical terms, a ground is the desirable return circuit path.

Check engine light - A dashboard warning light that is controlled by the vehicle computer; also called the *malfunction indicator light* or *MIL*.

Circuit - A circuit is the path that electrons travel from a power source, through a resistance, and back to the power source.

Circuit breaker - A mechanical unit that opens an electrical circuit in the event of excessive current flow.

Compressor - A device used in air-conditioning systems to raise the pressure and the temperature of the refrigerant.

Computer - Any device that can perform high-speed mathematical or logical calculations.

Computer command control (CCC or C^3) - The name of General Motors' computer engine control system for engines that use a carburetor.

Condenser - A radiator-like device used to condense the air-conditioning system refrigerant.

Conductor - A material that conducts electricity and heat. A metal that contains fewer than four electrons in its atom's outer shell.

Cone - The inner race or ring of a bearing.

Continuity - Instrument setup to check wiring, circuits, connectors, or switches for breaks (open circuit) or short circuits (closed circuit).

Controller - A name commonly used to describe a computer or an electronic control module.

Conventional theory - The theory that electricity flows from positive (+) to negative (-).

Coolant - The liquid mixture of antifreeze and water in the engine cooling system.

Corrosion - Wear by chemical or electrochemical reaction.

CRT - Cathode ray tube.

Cup - The outer race or ring of a bearing.

Current - Electron flow through an electrical circuit; measured in amperes.

Data - Information used as a basis for mechanical or electronic computation.

DC - Direct current.

DC coupling - A signal transmission that passes both AC and DC signal components to the meter.

Default setup - The setup that exists as long as there are no changes made to the settings.

Density – Mass per unit of volume; specific gravity.

Desiccant - A drying agent used in air-conditioning systems, usually silica alumina or silica gel.

Diagnostic trouble code (DTC) - An alphanumeric or numeric sequence indicating a fault in a vehicle operating system.

Dielectric strength - Resistance to electrical penetration.

Digital - A method of display that uses numbers instead of a needle or similar device.

Digital signal - An electrical signal that is either on or off with no in between.

Diode - An electrical device that allows current to flow in one direction only.

Direct current (DC) - A constant electric current that flows in one direction only.

Division - A specific segment of a waveform as defined by the grid on the display.

DOT - Abbreviation for the Department of Transportation.

DPDT switch - Double-pole, double-throw switch.

Duty cycle - On-time or off-time to period-time ratio expressed in a percentage.

Eccentric - The relationship of two round parts having different centers; a part which contains two round surfaces, not on the same center.

ECM - Electronic control module.

ECU - Electronic control unit.

EEPROM - Electronically erasable programmable read-only memory.

Elastomer - Another term for rubber.

Electricity - The movement of free electrons from one atom to another.

Electrode - A solid conductor through which current enters or leaves a substance, such as a gas or liquid.

Electrolyte - Any substance which, in solution, is separated into ions and is made capable of conducting an electric current; the acid solution of a lead-acid battery.

Electromagnetic induction - The generation of a current in a conductor that is moved through a magnetic field. Electromagnetic induction was discovered in 1831 by Michael Faraday.

Electromagnetic interference (EMI) - An undesirable electronic signal.

Electromagnetism - A magnetic field created by current flow through a conductor.

Electromotive force (EMF) - The force (pressure) that can move electrons through a conductor.

Electron - A negative-charged particle 1/1800 the mass of a proton.

Electron theory - The theory that electricity flows from negative (-) to positive (+).

Electronic circuit breaker - See *positive temperature coefficient.*

Element - Any substance that cannot be separated into different substances.

Emulsion – Dispersion of globules of one liquid in another.

Energy - Capacity for performing work.

Engine control module (ECM) - The on-board computer of the engine management system that controls fuel and emissions, as well as diagnostics, for the vehicle's engine management system.

Environmental Protection Agency (EPA) - A federal government agency that oversees the enforcement of laws related to the environment. Included in these laws are regulations on the amount and content of automotive emissions.

EPA - Environmental Protection Agency.

EPR - Ethylene propylene rubber; also an abbreviation of an air-conditioning valve called the *evaporator pressure regulator.*

EPROM - Erasable programmable read-only memory.

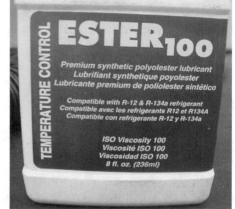

Ester oil - A type of refrigerant oil.

Evaporator - A radiator-like device used to absorb heat and cause the refrigerant to change from a liquid to a gas.

Farad - A unit of capacitance named for Michael Faraday (1791–1867), an English physicist. A farad is the capacity to store 1 coulomb of electrons at 1 volt of potential difference.

Fiber optics - The transmission of light through special plastic that keeps the light rays parallel even if the plastic is tied in a knot.

Foot-pound - A measurement of work. A one-pound load, moved one foot.

Freon - Dupont trade name for CFC-12 refrigerant.

Frequency - The number of times a waveform repeats in one second, measured in hertz (Hz), in a frequency band.

Friction - The resistance to sliding of two bodies in contact with each other.

Garter spring - A spring used in a seal to help keep the lip of the seal in contact with the moving part.

Gauge - Wire sizes as assigned by the American Wire Gauge system; the smaller the gauge number, the larger the wire.

Gauss - A unit of magnetic induction or magnetic intensity named for Karl Friedrich Gauss 1777 - 1855), a German mathematician.

Glitch - A momentary spike in a waveform. This can be caused by a momentary disruption in the tested circuit.

Gram - A metric unit of weight measurement equal to 1/1000 kilogram (1 gram × 28 = 1 oz.). An American dollar bill or paper clip weighs about 1 gram.

Grommet - An eyelet usually made from rubber used to protect, strengthen, or insulate around a hole or passage.

Ground - The lowest possible voltage potential in a circuit. In electrical terms, a ground is the desirable return circuit path. Ground can also be undesirable and provide a shortcut path for a defective electrical circuit.

Halogenated compounds - Chemicals containing chlorine, fluorine, bromine, or iodine. These chemicals are generally considered to be hazardous, and any product containing them should be disposed of using approved procedures.

Heat sink - Usually, a metallic-finned unit used to keep electronic components cool.

Hertz - A unit of measurement of frequency, abbreviated Hz. One hertz is one cycle per second. Named for Heinrich R. Hertz, a nineteenth century German physicist.

HFC-134a - Automotive air conditioning refrigerant, also called R-134a, whose chemical name is tetrofluorolthene.

High pressure switch - A switch used in an air-conditioning system to stop the operation of the compressor when the pressure reaches a dangerous level.

Horsepower - A unit of power equivalent to 33,000 foot-pounds per minute. One horsepower equals 746 W.

Hydroscopic - A term used to describe the absorption of water, especially from moisture in the air.

Intermittent - Irregular; a condition that happens with no apparent or predictable pattern.

ISO - International Standards Organization.

Kevlar - Dupont brand name of aramid fibers.

Kicker - A throttle kicker is used on some computer engine control systems to increase engine speed (RPM) during certain operating conditions, such as when the air-conditioning system is on.

Kilo - 1000; abbreviated k or K.

LCD - Liquid-crystal display.

LED - Light-emitting diode.

Liquid crystal display (LCD) - A display that uses liquid crystals to display waveforms and text on its screen.

Lock nut - See *prevailing torque nut*.

Low pressure switch - Used in an air-conditioning system to prevent the operation of the compressor when the pressure in the system is too low for safe operation.

Lubricant – Any substance introduced between two surfaces for the purpose of friction reduction.

Malfunction indicator lamp (MIL) - This amber dashboard warning light may be labeled "check engine" or "service engine soon."

Micron – Unit of measure equal to one millionth of a meter.

MIL - See *malfunction indicator lamp*.

Millisecond - One thousandth (1/1000) of one second.

Mineral oil – A refined hydrocarbon without animal or vegetable additives.

Miscible - A term that means "capable of being mixed."

Negative temperature coefficient (NTC) - Usually used in reference to a temperature sensor (coolant or air temperature). As the temperature increases, the resistance of the sensor decreases.

Nonvolatile memory - Computer memory capability that is not lost when power is removed. See also *read-only memory (ROM)*.

NTC - Negative temperature coefficient. Usually used in reference to a temperature sensor (coolant or air temperature). As the temperature increases, the resistance of the sensor decreases.

OE - Original equipment.

OEM - Original equipment manufacturer.

Ohm - The unit of electrical resistance; named for Georg Simon Ohm (1787–1854).

Ohmmeter - An electrical test instrument used to measure ohms (unit of electrical resistance).

Ohm's law - An electrical law that requires 1 volt to push 1 ampere through 1 ohm of resistance.

Ω (Omega) - The last letter of the Greek alphabet; a symbol for ohm, the unit for electrical resistance.

Open circuit - Any circuit that is not complete and in which no current flows.

Oscilloscope - A visual display of electrical waves on a fluorescent screen or cathode ray tube.

OSHA - Occupational Safety and Health Administration.

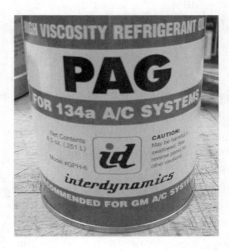

PAG - An abbreviation for polyalkeline glycol, an oil used in R134a automotive air conditioning systems.

Photoelectric principle - The production of electricity created by light striking certain sensitive materials, such as selenium or cesium.

POA - An abbreviation for an air-conditioning valve called the *pilot-operated absolute*.

Polarity - The condition of being positive or negative in relation to a magnetic pole.

Positive temperature coefficient (PTC) - Usually used in reference to a conductor or electronic circuit breaker. As the temperature increases, the electrical resistance also increases.

Potentiometer - A three-terminal variable resistor that varies the voltage drop in a circuit.

Power - In electrical terms, amperes × volts (Power = $I \times E$) expressed in watts.

Power train control module (PCM) - The on-board computer that controls both the engine management and transmission functions of the vehicle.

PPM - Parts per million.

PSI - Pounds per square inch.

PTC - See *positive temperature coefficient*.

Pulse - A voltage signal that increases or decreases from a constant value then returns to the original value.

R-12 - Air-conditioning refrigerant, also called CFC-12; the chemical name is diclorodifluoromethane.

R134a - Automotive air-conditioning refrigerant; also called HFC-134a; the chemical name is tetrafluorolthene.

Race - Inner and outer machined surface of a ball or roller bearing.

Receiver dryer - A device used as a reservoir and container for desiccant in some automotive air-conditioning systems.

Reference voltage - A voltage applied to a circuit.

Relative humidity - The percentage of water vapor in the air relative to the amount that could be in the air.

Relay - An electromagnetic switch that uses a movable arm.

Remanufactured - A term used to describe a component that is disassembled, cleaned, inspected, and reassembled using new or reconditioned parts. According to the Automotive Parts Rebuilders Association (APRA), this same component is also called *rebuilt*.

Renewal - A part built to be used as a replacement for the original equipment (OE) part.

Resistance - The opposition to current flow, measured in ohms.

Revolutions per minute (RPM) - A measure of how fast an object is rotating around an axis.

SAE - Society of Automotive Engineers.

Schrader valve - A spring-loaded valve used in the service ports of the fuel rail and air-conditioning system. Invented in 1844 by August Schrader.

Semiconductor - A material that is neither a conductor nor an insulator and has exactly four electrons in the atom's outer shell.

Shelf life - The length of time that something can remain on a storage shelf and not be reduced in performance level from that of a newly manufactured product.

Shim - A thin metal spacer.

Short circuit - A circuit in which current flows but bypasses some or all of the resistance in the circuit; a connection that results in a "copper-to-copper" connection.

Short to ground - A short circuit in which the current bypasses some or all of the resistance in the circuit and flows to ground. Because ground is usually steel in automotive electricity, a short to ground (grounded) is a "copper-to-steel" connection.

Society of Automotive Engineers (SAE) - A professional organization made up of automotive engineers and designers that establishes standards and conducts testing for many automotive-related functions.

Solenoid - An electromagnetic switch that uses a movable core.

Tell-tale light - Dash warning light (sometimes called an *idiot light*).

Thermistor - A resistor that changes resistance with temperature. A positive-coefficient thermistor has increased resistance with an increase in temperature. A negative-coefficient thermistor has increased resistance with a decrease in temperature.

Thermoelectric principle - The production of current flow created by heating the connection of two dissimilar metals.

Thermostat - A device that controls the flow in a system such as the engine cooling system based on temperature.

Throttle position (TP) sensor - A sensor that signals the computer as to the position of the throttle.

Torque - A twisting force measured in pounds-feet (lb-ft) or Newton-meters (N-m) that may or may not result in motion.

Torque wrench - A wrench that registers the amount of applied torque.

Torx - A type of fastener that features a star-shaped indentation for a tool. A registered trademark of the Camcar Division of Textron.

Transducer - An electrical and mechanical speed sensing and control unit used on cruise control systems.

Transistor - A semiconductor device that can operate as an amplifier or an electrical switch.

TXV - An abbreviation for an air-conditioning system that uses a thermostatic expansion valve.

Vacuum - Negative pressure (below atmospheric); measured in units of inches or centimeters of mercury (Hg).

Vacuum kicker - A computer-controlled throttle device used to increase idle RPM during certain operating conditions, such as when the air-conditioning system is operating.

Vacuum, manifold - Vacuum in the intake manifold that develops as a result of the intake stroke of the cylinders.

Vacuum, ported - A vacuum that develops on the intake side of the throttle plate as air moves past it.

Vehicle identification number (VIN) - Alphanumeric number identifying vehicle type, assembly plant, powertrain, etc.

VIR - An abbreviation of an old type of air-conditioning system in one unit called *valves in receiver*.

Volatility - A measurement of the tendency of a liquid to change to vapor.

Volt - The unit of measurement for the amount of electrical pressure; named for Alessandro Volta (1745–1827).

Voltage drop - Voltage loss across a wire, connector, or any other conductor. Voltage drop equals resistance in ohms times current in amperes (Ohm's law).

Voltmeter - An electrical test instrument used to measure volts (unit of electrical pressure). A voltmeter is connected in parallel with the unit or circuit being tested.

Watt - An electrical unit of power (1/746 hp); watts equal current (amperes) × voltage. Named after James Watt, a Scottish inventor.

WOT - Wide-open throttle.

Zener diode - A specially constructed (heavily doped) diode designed to operate with a reverse-bias current after a certain voltage has been reached. Named for Clarence Melvin Zener.

Zerk - A name commonly used for a grease fitting. Named in 1922 for its developer, Oscar U. Zerk, an employee of the Alemite Corporation. A grease fitting is also called an alemite fitting.

A7 Spanish-Language Glossary

Accumulator - acumulador - Un componente que está situado entre el compresor y el evaporador en el lado inferior del sistema. Este componente almacena el exceso de vapor refrigerante en un sistema de aire acondicionado que usa un tubo de orificio.

Align - alinear. Ponerse al lado. Poner partes de la unidad en la posición correcta.

Alloy - aleación. Metal que consta de un elemento o más que normalmente se añaden para aumentar la resistencia del metal base o darle propiedades importantes.

Alternator - alternador. Generador de corriente eléctrica que produce corriente alterna pero que se rectifica a la corriente directa por medio de diodos. También se llama *AC generator (generador de corriente alterna).*

Altitude - altitud. Distancia medida hasta la tierra al nivel del mar.

Ambient air temperature - temperatura ambiente. Temperatura del aire que rodea un objecto.

Ammeter - amperímetro/amperómetro/ametro. Instrumento eléctrico que sirve para medir amperios (unidad de la intensidad de corriente eléctrica).

Ampere - amperio. Unidad que mide la intensidad de corriente eléctrica. Llamada en honor de Andre Ampere (1775–1836).

Amplitude - amplitud. Diferencia entre la cresta y el valle de una onda.

Analog - análogo. Clase de instrumento del tablero de dirección/salpicadero que indica valores por medio del movimiento de un aguja o aparato parecido. Una señal análoga es continua y variable.

Anode - ánodo. Electrodo positivo hacia el cual fluyen los electrones.

ANSI (American National Standards Institute) - Instituto Nacional Americano de Estandares.

API (American Petroleum Institute) - Instituto Americano de Petróleo.

APRA (Automotive Parts Rebuilders Association) - Asociación de Reconstructores de Piezas Automotrices.

ASE (National Institute for Automotive Service Excellence) - Instituto Nacional de Excellencia de Servico Automotriz.

ASTM (American Society for Testing Materials) - Sociedad Americana para Materiales de Prueba.

Atom - átomo. La unidad más pequeña de materia que tiene características propias.

Atomize - atomizar. Reducir a o separar en partículas diminutas.

AWG (American wire gauge system) - sistema americano de calibrador de alambre.

Baffle - plato deflector. Plato o blindaje que se utiliza para desviar el flujo de o un líquido o un gas.

Bakelite - Marca de la Union Carbide Company para plástico de resina fenolformaldehida.

Barometric pressure - presión barométrica. Medida de presión atmosférica, en pulgadas de mercurio (Hg), que refleja la altitud y condiciones del tiempo.

Barrier hose - manguera o conducto de conexión estanca(o). Clase de manguera para un sistema de aire acondicionado que incluye una cubierta por dentro para prevenir la fuga de refrigerante por las paredes de la manguera. Normalmente se requiere el uso de mangueras barreras con refrigerante HFC-134a.

Base - base. Parte de un transistor que controla el flujo de corriente a través del transistor.

Battery - batería. Aparato químico que produce voltaje por medio de dos metales distintos sumergidos en un electrolito.

Baud rate - velocidad en baudios. Velocidad de trasmisión de las unidades de información en un flujo de datos en serie; se mide en bits por segundo.

Bidirectional communication - comunicación bidireccional. Comunicación por computadora que utiliza los datos en serie como ambas entrada y salida de datos.

Bit - bit/bitio. Señal de voltaje individual de un flujo de datos en serie; también la medida más pequeña que reconce la computadora.

Blower-motor - motor del ventilador. Motor eléctrico con un abanico que circula el aire dentro del automóvil para calentarlo, enfriarlo y descongelarlo.

BNC connector - conector BNC. Conector coaxial que normalmente se usa en los osciloscopios. Llamado en honor de su inventor, Baby Neil Councilman.

Brinelling - brinelling. Falla mecánica que describe una abolladura en metal, por ejemplo, la que ocurre cuando se aplica una carga a choque a un balero/cojinete. Llamado en honor de Johann A. Brinell, ingeniero sueco.

British thermal unit (BTU) - Unidad térmica británica. Calor necesario para elevar la temperatura de una libra de agua un grado Fahrenheit (°F) al nivel del mar.

Brushes - brochas/escobillas. Conductor de cobre o carbono que se utiliza para trasladar corriente eléctrica a o de una parte eléctrica que gira, como la que se encuentra en un motor o generador eléctrico.

Byte - byte/octeto. Ocho bits/bitios de información que se procesan como unidad y que se transmiten en sequencia en el flujo de datos en serie. También se llama *word (palabra)*.

Capacitance - capacidad. Mide la carga que puede almacenar un capacitor/condensador dado la diferencia de potencial de voltaje. Se mide en faradios o en incrementos más pequeños, como microfaradios.

Capacitor - capacitor. También se llama *condensor (condensador)*. Unidad eléctrica que puede trasladar corriente alterna pero que a la vez bloquear corriente directa; se usa en circuitos eléctricos para controlar las fluctuaciones de voltaje.

CCOT (cycling clutch orifice tube) - Abreviatura que se usa para identificar un sistema de aire acondicionado que emplea un tubo con orificio para ciclar el embrague.

Centi-Stoke – (cSt); centímetro por gramo por segundo; unidad de medición de la viscosidad de un fluído.

CFC-12 - Refrigerante del aire acondicionado; también se llama *R-12,* cuyo nombre químico es diclorodifluorometano.

Chassis - chasis. El bastidor, la suspensión, la dirección y la maquinaria de un automóvil.

Chassis ground - tierra de chasis. En términos eléctricos, una tierra es el camino deseable para el circuito de retorno.

Check engine light - luz de aviso del tablero controlada por la computadora del vehículo; también se llama *malfunction indicator light (MIL) la luz indicadora de mal funcionmiento.*

Circuit - circuito. Un circuito es el camino de los electrones: fluyen de un fuente de poder, a través de una resistencia y vuelven a la fuente de poder.

Circuit breaker - fusible interruptor de circuito. Unidad mecánica que abre un circuito eléctrico a caso de flujo de corriente en exceso.

Compressor - compresor. Mecanismo que se emplea en sistemas de aire acondicionado para aumentar la presión y la temperatura del refrigerante.

Computer - computadora. Mecanismo que puede realizar calculaciones matemáticas o lógicas de alta velocidad.

Computer command control (CCC or C3) - control por orden de computadora. El sistema de General Motors que consta de una computadora que controla el motor y que usa un carburador.

Condenser - condensador. Mecanismo como un radiador que se utiliza para condensar el refrigerante de un sistema de aire acondicionado.

Conductor - conductor. Material que conduce electricidad y calor. Un metal que tiene menos que cuatro electrones en el nivel más alejado del núcleo.

Cone - cono. El anillo de rodamiento interior de un cojinete.

Continuity - continuidad. Grupo de instrumentos que se usa para revisar alambrado, circuitos, conectores o interruptores para rupturas (circuito abierto) o corto circuito (circuito cerrado).

Controller - controlador. Nombre que se usa para describir una computadora o un módulo de control electrónico.

Conventional theory - teoría convencional. Teoriza que electricidad fluye de positivo (+) a negativo (–).

Coolant - agua de refrigeración/refrigerante. Mezcla líquida de anticongelante y agua en el sistema de enfriamiento del motor.

Corrosion - corrosión - Desgaste químico o por reacción electroquímica.

CRT (cathode ray tube) - Tubo de rayos catódicos.

Cup - copa. El anillo exterior de un balero.

Current - corriente. Flujo de electrones por un circuito eléctrico; se mide en amperios.

Data - datos. Información que se usa como base para computaciones mecánicas o eléctricas.

DC (direct current) - corriente directa.

DC (direct current) coupling - acoplador de corriente directa. Una transmisión de señal que pasa ambas las señales de AC y DC al instrumento de medida. *Véase también* AC coupling.

Default setup - sistema de defecto. Sistema que exista mientras que no haya cambios a los ajustes.

Density – densidad – Masa por unidad de volumen; peso específico.

Desiccant - secador. Material secador que se usa en sistemas de aire acondicionado, como aluminio silicio o gel silica.

Diagnostic trouble code (DTC) - código de falla. Sequencia alfanumérica o numérica que indica una falla en el sistema de funcionamiento de un vehículo.

Dielectric strength - resistencia diélectrica/potencial dieléctrico. Resistencia a la penetración eléctrica.

Digital - digital. Método de despliegue que utilza números en vez de una aguja o aparto parecido.

Digital signal - señal digital. Señal eléctrica que está o prendida o apagada sin otra opción.

Diode - diodo. Aparato eléctrico que permite que la corriente fluya en una sola dirección.

Direct current (DC) - corriente directa. Flujo constante de corriente eléctrica que fluye en una sola dirección.

Division - división. Segmento particular de una onda definido por la cuadrícula del despliegue.

DOT (Department of Transportation) - Abreviatura para el Departamento de Transportación.

DPDT (double-pole, double-throw) switch - conmutador bipolar de dos posiciones. Dos circuitos, dos posiciones.

Duty cycle - ciclo de duración. Porcentaje del período de un motor que el motor trabaja o reposa.

Eccentric - excéntrico. Relación de dos componentes redondos que tienen centros distintos; componente que tiene dos superficies redondos, que no se ubican en el mismo centro.

ECM (electronic control module) - módulo de control del motor.

ECU (electronic control unit) - unidad de control electrónica.

EEPROM (eletronically erasable programmable read-only memory) - memoria de acceso aleatorio programable y borrable electrónicamente.

Elastomer - cuacho/goma.

Electricity - electricidad. Movimiento de electrones libres de un átomo a otro.

Electrode - electrodo. Conductor sólido por lo cual corriente entra en o sale de una sustancia, así como un gas o un líquido.

Electrolyte - electrolito. Sustancia que, en solución, se separa en iones y se hace capaz de conducir una corriente eléctrica; la solución ácida de una batería de ácido-plomo.

Electromagnetic induction - inducción electromagnética. Generación de corriente en un conductor que pasa por un campo magnético. En 1831 Michael Faraday descubrió la inducción electromagnético.

Electromagnetic interference (EMI) - interferencia electromagnética. Señal electrónica indeseable.

Electromagnetism - electromagnetismo. Campo magnético creado por flujo de corriente por un conductor.

Electromotive force (EMF) - fuerza electromotriz. Fuerza (presión) que puede mover electrones por un conductor.

Electron - electrón. Partícula que lleva carga negativa y que tiene 1/1.800 la masa de un protón.

Electron theory - teoría de electrones. Teoría que dice que electricidad fluye desde negativo (–) a positivo (+).

Electronic circuit breaker - *Véase* PTC.

Element - elemento. Sustancia que no se puede separar en otras sustancias distintas.

Emulsion – emulsión – Dispersión de glóbulos de un líquido en otro.

Energy - energía. Capacidad para llevar al cabo trabajo.

Engine control module (ECM) - módulo de control del motor. Unidad de mando que controla el combustible y las emisiones, tal como diagnósticos.

Environmental Protection Agency (EPA) - Agencia de Protección del Medioambiente. Agencia del gobierno federal que impone las leyes que tienen que ver con el medio ambiente. Estas leyes incluyen las que reglamentan la cantidad y contenido de las emisiones automoviles.

EPA (Environmental Protection Agency) - agencia de protección ambiental.

EPR (ethylene propylene rubber) - caucho de etileno-propileno. También una abreviatura para la válvula del aire acondicionado que se llama *evaporator pressure regulator (válvula reguladora de la presión del evaporador).*

EPROM (erasable programmable read-only memory) - memoria de sólo lectura borrable y programable.

Ester oil - aceite ester. Clase de aceite refrigerante.

Evaporator - evaporador. Mecanísmo parecido a un radiador que se usa para absorber calor y para hacer que el refrigerante cambie de líquido a gas.

Farad - faradio. Unidad de capacidad. Llamado en honor de Michael Faraday (1791–1867), físico inglés. Un faradio es la capacidad de almacenar 1 coulomb de electrones a 1 voltio de diferencia de potencial.

Fiber optics - transimisión por fibra óptica. Transmisión de luz por medio de un plástico especial que mantiene los rayos paralelos aún cuando el plástico se anuda.

Foot-pound - libras pies/pie-libra. Medida del esfuerzo de rotación. Una fuerza de una libra aplicada sobre un objeto a una distancia de un pie desde el centro de dicho objeto.

Freon - Freon. Marca de Dupont para refrigerante CFC-12.

Frequency - frequencia. Número de veces una onda se repite en un segundo, que se mide en Hertz (Hz), en una banda.

Friction - fricción. Resistencia al deslizamiento entre dos objetos en contacto.

Garter spring - muelle/bobina toroidal. Resorte usado en un cierre para ayudar mantener el labio del sello en el contacto con la parte móvil.

Gauge - calibrador. Calibres de alambre asignados por el sistema americano del calibrador de alambre; lo más pequeño el número del calibrador, lo más grande el alambre.

Gauss - gauss. Unidad de inducción o intensidad magnética llamada en honor de Karl Friedrich Gauss (1777–1855), un matemático alemán.

Glitch - fallo técnico. Cresta momentánea en una onda. Puede ser resulta de una interrupción momentánea en el circuito probado.

Gram - gramo. Unidad métrica de la medida del peso igual a un 1/1000 de un kilogramo (28 gramos = 1 onza). Un dólar americano o un clip pesa alrededor de 1 gramo.

Grommet - arandela. Un ojete generalmente hecho de caucho que se usa para proteger, reforzar o aislar alrededor de un hoyo o pasaje.

Ground - tierra. Potencial posible más bajo del voltaje en un circuito. En términos eléctricos, tierra es el sendero deseable de circuito de regreso. Tierra puede ser también indeseable y puede proporcionar un sendero del atajo para un circuito eléctrico defectuoso.

Halogenated compounds - compuestos halogenados. Sustancias químicas que contienen cloro, flúor, bromo o yodo. Estas sustancias químicas generalmente se consideran peligrosas y cualquier producto que las contiene debe ser deshecho según procedimientos aprobados.

Heat sink - absorbente de calor. Generalmente, una unidad de metal con planos de derive que se usa para mantener frescos los componentes electrónicos.

Hertz - hertz. Unidad de la medida de la frecuencia, abreviada Hz. Un Hertz es un ciclo por segundo. Llamado en honor de Heinrich R. Hertz, físico alemán del siglo diecinueve.

HFC-134a - Refrigerante automotriz de aire acondicionado, que también se llama R-134a, cuyo nombre químico es tetrafluoroétano.

High pressure switch - interruptor alta presión. Interruptor que se usa en un sistema de aire acondicionado para parar la operación del compresor cuando la presión alcance un nivel peligroso.

Horsepower - caballo de fuerza. Unidad de fuerza equivalente a 33,000 librapies por minuto. Un caballo de fuerza iguala 746 W.

Hydroscopic - hidroscópico. Término que se usa para describir la absorción de agua especialmente de humedad en el aire.

Intermittent - intermitente. Irregular; una condición que acontece sin una pauta fija, aparente o previsible.

ISO (Internationl Standards Organization) - Organización Internacional de Estándares.

Kevlar - Kevlar. Marca de Dupont de fibras aramida.

Kicker - disparador. Se usa un disparador de válvula de admisión en algunos sistemas de control electrónicos para aumentar la velocidad (RPM) de motor durante ciertas condiciones de funcionamiento, tal como cuando el sistema de aire acondicionado está activado.

Kilo - kilo. 1.000; se abrevia «k» o «K».

LCD (liquid crystal display) - VCL. Visualizador de cristal líquido.

LED (light-emitting diode) - diodo luminoso.

Liquid crystal display (LCD) - visualizador de cristal líquido (VCL). Visualizador que usa cristales líquidos para desplagar ondas y texto en la pantalla.

Lock nut - tuerca de seguridad. *Véase* prevailing torque nut.

Low pressure switch - interruptor de baja presión. Se usa en un sistema de aire acondicionado para prevenir la operación del compresor cuando la presión en el sistema es demasiado baja para la operación segura.

Lubricant – lubricante - Cualquier sustancia que se coloca entre dos superficies con el objetivo de reducir la fricción entre ambas**.**

Malfunction indicator lamp (MIL) - luz/lámpara de indicación de problemas/fallas. Esta luz ámbar de advertir que se ubica en el tablero/salpicadero puede llevar el nombre *check engine* o *service engine soon.*

Micron – micra - Unidad de medida que equivale a una millonésima de un metro (o milésima de un milímetro).

MIL - *Véase* malfunction indicator lamp.

Millisecond - milisegundo. Un milésimo de un segundo (1/1000).

Mineral oil – aceite mineral - Un hidrocarbono refinado sin aditivos animales o vegetales.

Miscible - miscible. Término que significa «capaz de ser mezclado».

Negative temperature coefficient (NTC) - coeficiente de temperatura negativo. Generalmente que se usa en referencia a un sensor de la temperatura (líquido refrigerante o temperatura aérea). Mientras que la temperatura se aumenta, la resistencia del sensor se disminuye.

Nonvolatile memory - memoria permanente. Memoria de la computadora que no se pierde cuando se apaga. *Véase también* read-only memory (ROM).

NTC (negative temperature coefficient) - coeficiente de temperatura negativo. Generalmente que se usa en referencia a un sensor de la temperatura (líquido refrigerante o temperatura aérea). Mientras que la temperatura se aumenta, la resistencia del sensor se disminuye.

OE (original equipment) - equipo original.

OEM (original equipment manufacturer) - fabricante de equipo original.

Ohm - ohmio. Unidad de la resistencia eléctrica; llamada en honor de Georg Simon Ohm (1787–1854).

Ohmmeter - ohmiómetro. Instrumento de prueba eléctrico que se usa para medir los ohmios (unidad de la resistencia eléctrica).

Ohm's law - ley de Ohm. Ley eléctrica que dice que se necesita 1 voltio para mover 1 amperio por 1 ohmio de resistencia.

Ω (omega) - omega. Última letra del alfabeto griego; símbolo para el ohmio (Ω), la unidad de resistencia eléctrica.

Open circuit - circuito abierto. Circuito que no es completo y por lo cual no corriente fluye.

Oscilloscope - osciloscopio. Despliegue visual de ondas eléctricas en una pantalla fluorescente o en un tubo de rayos catódicos.

OSHA (Occupational Safety and Health Administration) - Instituto de Seguridad e Higiene en el Trabajo.

PAG (polyalkilene glycol) - Abreviatura para *glicoles polialquilenos.*

Photoelectric principle - principio fotoeléctrico. Producción de electricidad creada por la luz al atacar ciertas materias sensibles, tal como selenio o cesio.

POA (pilot–operated absolute) - Abreviatura para una válvula de aire acondicionado que se llama válvula piloto de regulación de presión absoluta.

Polarity - polaridad. Condición de ser positivo o negativo con relación a un polo magnético.

Positive temperature coefficient (PTC) - coeficiente de temperatura positivo. Generalmente se usa en referencia a un conductor o fusible interruptor de circuito electrónico. Mientras la temperatura aumenta, la resistencia eléctrica también se aumenta.

Potentiometer - potenciómetro. Resistor variable de tres terminales que varía la caída del voltaje en un circuito.

Power - poder. En términos eléctricos, voltios por amperios (poder = I × E) que se expresa en vatios.

Power train control module (PCM) - módulo de control del tren de fuerza. Computador en el vehículo que controla ambas la regulación del motor y las funciones de la transmisión.

PPM (parts per million) - partes por millón.

PSI (pounds per square inch) - libras por pulgada cuadrada.

PTC - *Véase* positive temperature coefficient.

Pulse - pulso. Señal de voltaje que aumenta o disminuye desde un valor constante y después vuelve al valor original.

R-12 - Refrigerante del aire acondicionando que se llama también CFC-12; el nombre químico es diclorodifluorométano.

R134a - Refrigerante del aire acondicionando automotriz que se llama también HFC-134a; el nombre químico es tetrafluoroletileno.

Race - pista de rodamiento. Superficie interior y exterior fresada de un cojinete de bolas o de rodillas.

Receiver dryer - receptor secador. Artefacto que se usa como un depósito y contenedor para el secador en unos sistemas de aire acondicionado automotrices.

Reference voltage - voltaje de referencia– Voltaje que se aplica a un circuito.

Relative humidity - humedad relativa. Porcentaje de vapor de agua que podría estar en el aire comparado con la cantidad verdadera en el aire.

Relay - relevador. Interruptor electromagnético que usa un brazo movible.

Remanufactured - reconstruido. Término que se usa para describir un componente que se desmonta, se limpia, se inspecciona y se vuelve a montar utilizando repuestos nuevos o rehabilitados. Según la Automotive Parts Rebuilders Association (APRA), este componente mismo también se llama *rebuilt*.

Renewal - recambio o pieza de recambio. UNA parte construida para ser usado como un repuesto para la parte del equipo original (OE).

Resistance - resistencia. Oposición al flujo de corriente que se mide en ohmios.

Revolutions per minute (RPM) - revoluciones por minuto. Medida de cuán rapidamente un objeto gira sobre un eje.

SAE (Society of Automotive Engineers) - Sociedad de Ingenieros Automotrices.

Schrader valve - válvula schrader. Válvula cargada de resorte que se usa en los puertos de servicio del riel del combustible y el sistema de aire acondicionado. Inventado en 1844 por August Schrader.

Semiconductor - semiconductor. Materia que es ni conductor ni aislador y que tiene exactamente cuatro electrones en el nivel exterior de átomo.

Shelf life - tiempo de durabilidad antes de la venta. Plazo de tiempo que algo puede permanecer en un estante de almacenamiento sin que el nivel de desempeño se reduzca del desempeño de un producto que se acaba de fabricar.

Shim - lámina de ajuste. Espaciador de metal delgado.

Short circuit - circuito corto. Circuito en que la corriente fluye pero evita un poco de o toda la resistencia en el circuito; una conexión que tiene como resultado una conexión «cobre a cobre».

Short to ground - corto a tierra. Circuito corto por lo cual la corriente fluye pero evita algo de o toda la resistencia en el circuito y fluye a tierra. Porque el suelo es generalmente acero en la electricidad automotriz, un corto a tierra (puesto a tierra) es una conexión «cobre a acero».

Society of Automotive Engineers (SAE) - Sociedad de Ingenieros Automotrices. Organización profesional compuesta de ingenieros y diseñadores automotrices que establece estándares y que hace pruebas para muchas funciones qie tienen que ver con el automóvil.

Solenoid - solenoide. Interruptor electromagnético que usa un núcleo movible.

Tell-tale light - lámpara de aviso. Lámpara de advertir del tablero (a veces se llama *idiot light (luz de idiota).*

Thermistor - termistor. Resistor que varía su resistencia según la temperatura. Un termistor de coeficiente positivo aumenta la resistencia cuando se aumenta la temperatura. Un termistor de coeficiente negativo aumenta la resistencia con una disminución de temperatura.

Thermoelectric principle - principio termoeléctrico. Producción del flujo de corriente creado calentando la conexión de dos metales distintos.

Thermostat - termostato. Artefacto que controla el flujo en un sistema basado en la temperatura tal como el sistema de refrigeración de motor.

Throttle position (TP) sensor - sensor del ángulo de apertura del acelerador. Sensor que indica la posición del acelerador a la computadora.

Torque - torque/torsión. Fuerza que tuerce que se mide en libras pies (lb-ft) o Newton–metros (N–m), que pueda resultar en movimiento.

Torque wrench - llave de tensión. Llave inglesa que registra la cantidad de torsión que se aplica.

Torx - tipo de cierre que tiene una endedura en forma de estrella para una herramienta. Una marca registrada de la División Camcar de Textron.

Transducer - transductor. Unidad de control eléctrica y mecánica que presiente la velocidad que se usa en sistemas de control de crucero.

Transistor - transistor. Artefacto semiconductor que puede operar como amplificador o interruptor eléctrico.

TXV (thermostatic expansion valve) - Abreviatura para un sistema de aire acondicionando que usa una válvula de expansión termostática.

Vacuum - vacío. Presión negativa (menos que la presión atmosférica); se mide en pulgadas o centímetros de mercurio (Hg).

Vacuum kicker - disparador de vacío. Mecanismo de la válvula de admisión controlado por la computadora que se usa para aumentar RPM de marcha mínima durante ciertas condiciones de operación, tal como durante la operación del sistema de aire acondicionando.

Vacuum, manifold - depresión de admisión. Vacío en el múltiple de admisión que desarrollo como resultado de la carrera de admisión de los cilíndros.

Vacuum, ported - vacío de puerto. Vacío que desarrolla en el lado de admisión de la mariposa del acelerador cuando el aire la pasa.

Vehicle identification number (VIN) - número de identificación de vehículo. Número alfanumérico que identifica el tipo del vehículo, la planta de ensamblaje, el tren de potencia etc.

VIR - Una abreviación de un antiguo tipo de sistema de aire acondicionado en una unidad, llamado *valves in receiver (válvulas en el receptor).*

Volatility - volatilidad. Medida de la tendencia de un líquido para cambiar al vapor.

Volt - voltio. Unidad para la cantidad de presión eléctrica; llamado en honor de Alessandro Volta (1745–1827).

Voltage drop - caída de tensión. Pérdida de voltaje a través de un alambre, conector o cualquier otro conductor. La caída de tensión es la resistencia en ohmios por la corriente en amperios (la ley del Ohmio).

Voltmeter - voltímetro. Instrumento eléctrico de la prueba que se usa para medir los voltios (la unidad de la presión eléctrica). El voltímetro se conecta en paralelo con la unidad o el circuito que se está probando.

Watt - vatio. Unidad eléctrica de poder; un vatio (1/746 hp) iguala el voltaje por la corriente (amperios). Llamado en honor de James Watt, inventor escocés.

WOT (wide-open throttle) - acelerador a plenos gases.

Zener diode - diodo-Zener. Diode especialmente construido (muy dopado) diseñado para operar con una corriente de corriente de retorno después de que se alcance un cierto voltaje. Llamado en honor de Clarence Melvin Zener.

Zerk - Zerk. Nombre que se usa comúnmente para una grasera. Llamado en 1922 en honor de su diseñador, Oscar U. Zerk, un empleado de la Corporación Alemite. Una grasera también se llama *Alemite fitting*.

Index